# The Hypnotic Handshakes

# The

# Hypnotic

# Handshakes

## by Graham Old

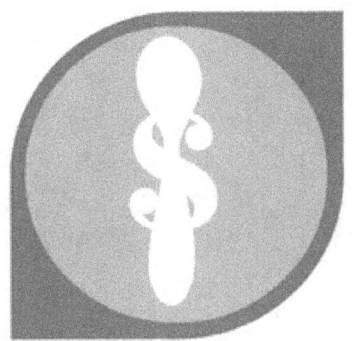

The Hypnotic Handshakes

## Preface

This book is the fourth instalment in our *Inductions Masterclass* series. If you have read any of the previous books in the series, you will know that our aim is to take a popular induction and devote an entire book to discussing its practice.

This title in the series is a slight deviation in that we are teaching three inductions in one book. So, *The Hypnotic Handshakes* will present and unpack three different handshake inductions: The Bandler Handshake, the Elman Handshake and the Erickson Handshake (otherwise known as *the ambiguous touch*).

As with its predecessors, this book takes the inductions as a starting-point and uses them to teach a number of principles that are beneficial for the wider practice of hypnosis.

Our intention, as always, is incredibly simple: we seek to take inductions that work and enable you to work with them. With handshake inductions it may seem as if live training or video instruction would be more effective than a book. However, whilst we acknowledge that being able to demonstrate visually what we are describing would be helpful, our hope is that each book in this series will be as close to live training as you can get, from the comfort of your own home! We are aiming to replicate the level, detail and quality of information you will receive at a live training. Therefore, we aim to anticipate questions from the Floor, as well as handle all the natural diversions and meandering discussions that often take place.

We conduct live training events ourselves, so know how valuable they can be. However, it can be frustrating to get home and feel like you have forgotten something, or find the course notes a bit slim, or fail to read your own handwriting! With this book, you are free to read and re-

read it time and time again.

There are no shortage of videos online demonstrating these inductions, so you can access them for free. However, we wanted to be able to devote an entire book to some of the often overlooked elements in handshake inductions, that might be skipped over in videos. Additionally, most hypnosis videos online only show the successes. Yet, no one learns an induction once and then executes it perfectly every single time. Therefore, the longest and most valuable chapter in this book may be the Trouble-Shooting one, which you are encouraged to return to as you keep practising the hypnotic handshakes.

## Terminology used

Throughout this book you will find us referring to 'trance' and at times using terminology such as 'subconscious,' being 'under' or 'in' hypnosis, deepening, and so on. Please bear in mind that we are using these as phenomenological descriptions, merely meant to convey what the hypnotee may be experiencing. We are not endorsing any particular interpretation of hypnosis, or taking sides in the perennial debates over the nature of trance or the existence of a special hypnotic state.

For more on our experiential model of hypnosis, which fits comfortably with all of the major schools of Hypnosis, see our introductory Book, '*The Anatomy of Inductions.*'

## Acknowledgements

Grateful acknowledgement is given to Jon Chase, from whom I first learned a version of the handshake induction. Additionally, I am grateful to John Cleesattel for discussions had regarding his model of hypnosis and expectancy and for granting permission for us to share his version of an expectancy induction.

## All Rights Reserved

## Disclaimer

# Contents

# Introduction

For many people, handshake inductions are the epitome of hypnotic ritual. They are the quintessential expected behaviour of one deemed to be a hypnotist. They both demonstrate the speed with which a skilled hypnotist can "entrance" his "subject," and the ease with which said subjects can slip into hypnosis.

However there is no single induction known as the handshake induction. Instead, there are at least four, three of which we will focus on in this book. In fact, if you consider that most Hypnosis or NLP Trainers may add their preferred slant onto whatever handshake induction they are teaching, it may be more accurate to say that there are hundreds if not thousands of versions of the hypnotic handshake.

The most famous of the handshake inductions may actually be the one we are not devoting any space to. This is the technique where a Stage Hypnotist will go to shake someone's arm and then pull it as they command, "Sleep!" You can see our reasoning for avoiding this technique in the Trouble-Shooting chapter.

## Why Learn the Hypnotic Handshakes?

There are a few reasons why learning handshake inductions is a valuable investment of time and energy for the budding hypnotist.

Firstly, as suggested, they are precisely the kind of manoeuvre that some people will be expecting from a so-called hypnotist. Like it or not, for some people, you will not be considered a valid or reputable hypnotist unless you can pull-off the kind of behaviours that they have learned from watching stage and television versions of hypnosis.

You can invest your energy in teaching people that there is a natural difference between stage hypnosis and the kind of work that you do, but you might want to consider why you would be doing that? If someone is already primed to think that if you act in a certain way, then they will react in a particular way, why not use that to your advantage? It is almost as if someone has said to you, "If you do so-and-so, I will know it is real hypnosis and will therefore respond in such-a-way..." Do you really want to miss that opportunity?

The second reason for learning the Handshake inductions is that they are an incredibly flexible tool. In fact, one of the reasons that we have structured this book the way that we have is because if the first one does not work for you, then you can seamlessly move into one of the other inductions (Elman and Erickson) that follow.

However, even if you choose to stick with the Bandler handshake, we will describe five different ways that the induction can be approached. In effect, we are giving you 4 or 5 'outs' – different directions that you can go in, depending on how your partner responds.[1] Although some descriptions of this induction make it sound like a very regimented series of steps that need to be followed exactly, you will learn that the induction has been an exercise in flexibility from the very beginning.

Thirdly, yet not unrelated to the point above, this induction is worth learning because of the amount of feedback that it provides the hypnotist. You will learn how easily your partner responds with 'automatic' movements. You will make physical contact, allowing you to feel the warmth or cold in their hand. You will also feel the weight of their hand, demonstrating whether a weighty relaxation or floating catalepsy are the most appropriate end to be aimed for.

---

1   We much prefer the description 'partner' to 'subject.' Ordinarily, we would choose, 'client.' However, as this induction often attracts those from a Stage or Street Hypnosis background, we felt it useful to introduce a new term.

GRAHAM OLD

# The Bandler Handshake

The following chapter aims to meet two possibly contradictory ends. On the one hand, we want to demonstrate that the oft-revered Bandler Handshake induction is generally incredibly simple (and not the kind of thing you need an entire book to teach!). On the other hand, we hope to demonstrate that there are all sorts of variables and intended outcomes, which mean that this is less about learning an individual hypnosis induction and more about adopting skills that enable you to be more hypnotic.

We will begin by looking at the nature of the Bandler handshake and offering a further reason for studying it. We will consider what it is that the induction aims to do and how it intends to do it. At that point, we will turn to a straightforward example of the induction in action. Then, in the chapters that follow, we will look at five different variations of the Bandler handshake. You will soon learn that, on the one hand, there is less mystery or mastery here than many youtube videos may lead you to conclude and on the other hand, this is far more than simply interrupting a handshake and pointing to their hand.

## Whose Handshake?

Originally, Richard Bandler credited Milton Erickson with the handshake that follows. However, in later years he has given various reasons why he did so. Sometimes, he suggests that he simply wanted to pay homage to one of his early influences. At other times, he states that Erickson's ideas and behaviour inspired the handshake that Bandler himself developed.

One of the reasons that Bandler now gives for stating that Erickson did not invent the induction is that Erickson's condition of Polio would have prevented him from executing the kind of movements that this induction involves. However, this strikes us as an unlikely preventative factor.

It is a matter of record that Erickson's polio worsened as he got older. Moreover, it is not the type of condition that merely moves in one direction. That is, it is entirely possible that Erickson may have been able to perform an induction on one day that he could not on the next. Yet, perhaps a week later, he may briefly have been able to perform it again.

Nevertheless, there is no denying that it is Bandler who popularised this induction. It is also clear that it owes its genesis to Erickson's *Ambiguous Touch* handshake, which we will turn to later. Therefore, for the sake of classification, we are happy to describe this as the Bandler Handshake, whilst later paying homage to what may undoubtedly be referred to as the Erickson Handshake, otherwise known as *the ambiguous touch*.

Having said that, handshake inductions were popular in hypnosis long before either Erickson or Bandler appeared on the scene. As we unpack how the inductions work, the reasons why may become clear. At the very least, they can appear dramatic and therefore 'hypnotic,' whilst generally being fairly straightforward to perform.

## Why Learn the Bandler Handshake?

In the Introduction we gave three reasons for learning handshake inductions. However, there is a fourth reason that we are allocating the majority of this book to the Bandler Handshake. That is because we believe that by learning this induction you will be practising hypnosis in a nutshell.

If you have read our earlier e-book, *The Anatomy of Inductions*, then you will know that we define hypnosis in experiential terms. We describe it as, 'An imagination-fuelled, creatively engaged, shift in a person's perception of the world & their relationship to it.' Additionally, we suggest that all effective hypnotic inductions contain the following 5 elements, to some degree:

1. Gain Consent / Get Contract
2. Create expectancy
3. Absorb attention / awareness
4. Engage the imagination
5. Arouse emotions / feelings

We would go so far as to suggest that an effective handshake induction may contain all 5 of these elements and, as such, is a perfect way to model an experiential understanding of hypnosis.

Simply by shaking your hand, your partner has given

an element of consent. Then, the surprise of having you interrupt the handshake by taking hold of their wrist, can amplify any expectancy already present. They literally wait for you to tell them what is going on.

As you focus their eyes on their hand, you absorb their attention and – through your suggestions – engage their imagination.

The final element is to simply arouse their emotions. The simple act of interrupting their handshake will create excitement for some people. Additionally, the words you use to engage their imagination – speaking of the benefits of what they are experiencing – will likely arouse further emotions and feelings.

**What does it look like?**

We will discuss the induction – and various versions of it – in more detail below. For now, a simple description will suffice:

- You begin by appearing to initiate a handshake

- As your partner enters into the handshake, your other hand takes hold of the wrist of the arm they put forward

- You lift their hand up so that it is in front of their face, palm facing them

- Tell them to focus on their hand

- You tell them that as their hand draws closer to

18

their face, they can notice the changing focus of their eyes...

- And their eyes can close...

- As their hand touches their face...

- And they go deep inside.

We will look at the subject of deepeners in the next chapter.

# GRAHAM OLD

# EXERCISE

Practice *not* shaking hands. I am not necessarily thinking of the old prank where someone goes to shake your hand and you move it away to brush your hair, though that would be an example.

You might wait until your partner has offered their hand, then move your hand to pat your pocket. "Sorry, I thought that was my phone..."

Or you could retract your hand as they go to shake it, as you rub your shoulder and say, "Ooh, something really clicked there."

Do this as often as you can. Over time, you will get an idea of the kind of time-scale involved in moving your hand away. You will also notice that some people's hands will stay resting in the air for a few seconds after you move yours. You will also gain an appreciation for how automatically people tend to respond to a potential hand-shake.

GRAHAM OLD

# The Floating Hand

This version of the induction is one of the most popular. Some people find this the easiest version to start with, perhaps because on the surface it appears to require minimal input from the hypnotist, whilst providing a significantly powerful experience for their partner.

It is actually far more difficult to explain this induction, than it is to perform it. The reason for this is precisely because it really is as straightforward as it seems.

You reach out to initiate a handshake. Your partner responds, as expected, by offering their hand for the shake. Just as your fingers are about to touch (or even in the split-second after they have), you take hold of their wrist with your other hand.

Now, you lift their arm up such that their palm is facing them, their fingers approximately level with their nose or eye-line. You simultaneously direct their attention, by pointing at their hand and then continue with patter like so:

"Look at that hand."

[Point at the hand]

"Just look at that hand and notice as that hand

begins to want to move towards you..."

[You may notice the hand moving of its own accord. Otherwise, you can gently and – this is important – *imperceptibly* move it towards them to get it started.]

"That's it... And as that hand moves towards your face...

"You can notice the changing focus of your eyes and note the tendency for your eyes to close..."

[Slightly move your hand in front of their face and point downwards as you say, "eyes to close."]

"As you notice that hand getting closer and closer to your face...

"That's right, closer and closer, all the way down, until you just allow it to happen...all the way down...that's right...all the way down now as that hand reaches your face..."

[Or if their eyes have not yet closed:]

"That's right, closer and closer, all the way down... Now go ahead and take a nice deep breath... And as you breathe out allow your eyes to close, until you just allow it to happen...all the way down...that's right...all the way down now as that hand reaches your face..."

# THE HYPNOTIC HANDSHAKES

It is natural to follow this up with a deepener. The most natural deepener, given the position of their hand, is to associate the intensification of their current experience with their hand falling down to their side. That may look something like this:

> "And you won't *go all of the way into hypnosis* until your hand happens to fall all of the way down."

> [Continue the patter until their arm/hand has fallen completely to their side, or onto their lap. An example might be:]

> "As that hand continues to drift down in its own time, you can find yourself drifting deeper into that experience... And you may not have known that you had this ability to access that deep resourceful subconscious state of yours, quite so easily... Yet, now that you have, you may see, or experience or simply know the solutions to all of those issues that have been troubling you. You may or may not yet know how to get there from here, but you will find yourself increasingly knowing exactly where it is that you want to go..."

> [Once the arm/hand has reached their side or lap, you can of course continue intensifying their experience:]

> "And in a moment, I will take your arm and just drop it by your side, allowing you to go twice as deep...

[Lift up their arm by the wrist. It should feel heavy, as if you are doing all of the lifting. If it does not, shake it slightly from side to side, as if you are relaxing it further. Then allow the arm to drop down.]

"And in a moment, I will take your [other] arm and just drop it by your side, finding yourself going deeper still, deeper, deeper, deepest...
all the way down..."

[Lift up their other arm by the wrist. Then allow the arm to drop down.]

It is possible to make this induction seem far more complex than it is. The only reason we are dedicating so much space to it is to cover every eventuality. In short, the induction really is as simple as:

1.  Look at your hand...

2.  As that hand moves towards your face
    [On its own, or with assistance...]

3.  Your eyes will begin to change focus

4.  And when you become aware of your eyes
    [wave hand down in front of eyes...]

5.  Close your eyes

6.  And sleep...

# THE HYPNOTIC HANDSHAKES

## Moving their Hand Towards their Face

The key with this version of the induction is the hand moving up or towards their face. However, before we look at two ways to achieve this, I need to make a slight detour to say a little bit about your hand placement:

When you hold their hand up in front of their face, my recommendation is to do so with minimal contact. If you hold their arm too firmly, then you will be unlikely to notice how much strength they are, or are not, putting into the process. Instead, think of yourself as someone skilled in tai-chi, aikido or wing chun. Your aim is to sense the slightest movement, or direction of energy, before they themselves are even aware of it.

The best way to achieve this is to hold their arm lightly. I usually aim to hold their wrist between my thumb and middle finger, with my forefinger on the back of their hand. This position provides me with the best feedback, in terms of how much strength or resistance is being put into the movement. Then, once I am confident that the hand is staying up, I can even let go with my middle finger and thumb, meaning that I am only keeping contact via my index finger on the back of their hand.]

Now, back to the hand-to-head movement! There are two ways that this may take place.

Firstly, you may rely simply upon the power of suggestion. In that sense, this induction is akin to something like magnetic hands. You might use patter like

27

the following:

> "As you become aware of your head pulling that hand like a magnet, you might notice the tendency for your hand to be drawn towards your face. Your hand finding itself irresistibly drawn towards your face... your head almost trying to resist the pull to fall forwards as you become aware of that inevitable attraction, that magnetic pull between your hand and your head... feeling exactly as you would expect it to feel if there were magnets in your fingertips pulled towards your magnetic forehead..."

Until you try it, you may be surprised how often this actually works!

The key here is that you are not only telling your partner what is about to take place, although it may feel like that to them. Instead, you are sensing what is happening in the split-second before they do and then announcing it. The execution of your announced action reinforces their belief in your capabilities and increases the likelihood of them responding to further suggestions.

In this case, as you hold their hand in front of their face, you can become aware of how heavy or compliant it feels. With practice, you will get a sense of whether or not this hand will move by sheer suggestion alone. If you feel that it will, then you can proceed as above, using the idea of the hand and forehead being magnetised. If the hand feels heavy, or less likely to move of its own accord, then you may wish to proceed to the second option.

The second means of achieving hand-movement is remarkably simple: if the hand does not move on its own, you move it! I am not suggesting that you push their hand. If you do so, they are likely to feel this and resist.

However, If your forefinger is on the back of their hand, maintaining contact, whilst refusing to move *away* from their face, you will inevitably get the movement you require. It is only natural that over time your partner's hand will move slightly. If it moves away from their face, it will be stopped by your forefinger. If it moves towards their face, even if just by millimetres, it will do so freely. Yet, because you are keeping contact with the back of their hand, your forefinger will also move forward. The result is that their hand will find a new resting place, slightly forward of its previous position.

The result of this, over time, is that you will be imperceptibly moving their hand closer and closer to their face, as your pacing and leading sounds like prophetic suggestion and they conclude that the movement is merely a result of your instructions. Once the suggestion really takes, helped perhaps by your "magnetic" patter, you can even let the hand move away from your finger, as you keep your hand still and they continue to move closer to their face.

# GRAHAM OLD

# EXERCISE

Spend some time watching online videos of people performing "the Bandler handshake."

The chances are that you will come across a whole host of variations!

Bear in mind, that online videos tend to only show someone's success with an induction. However, as you watch the videos, note any interesting elements that you think are useful.

It may be that you discover content that contradicts or supersedes what you read in this book. That, of course, is perfectly fine.

GRAHAM OLD

# The Falling Hand

Although it can seem as if this variation involves more work than the floating hand, the reverse is actually true. Additionally, we have found that if we start by aiming for this, then we are best-placed to divert towards one of the other variations.

This may be an extension of the floating hand, where the hand naturally floats *down* to the face, helped by gravity. Or it may be a variation of the frozen hand, where the hand is originally cataleptic and then deepens trance as it falls *to their side*. Either way, your role is to convey the idea that whatever takes place is doing so due to your suggestions and their powerful mind.

Like much hypnotic phenomena (for example, magnetic hands), the natural physiological outcomes are skilfully reinterpreted to serve the purposes of the hypnotist. A wonderful example of this is the thumb-stare induction, which is an almost identical process to that seen in this variation.[2]

The different headings in this section may make it seem as if you need to start out your induction with one of these variations in mind. That, however, is not how I operate. Instead, I like to think of the different variations as possible exit ramps. Personally, I begin by usually

---

2   See http://www.howtodoinductions.com/inductions/thumb

heading towards this variation then, depending on the reactions I get, I might veer off into one of the other variations at the appropriate point.

As you hold their hand in front of their face, instructing them to look at it, you will notice the feeling of the hand. If you hold the wrist too tightly, you will not do so. Instead, as stated, I prefer to hold it *lightly* between my thumb and middle finger, with my forefinger on the back of the hand. In my experience, this seems to give the highest level of feedback.

However, even before this point there is an opportunity to sense-and-respond to your partner. In that split second between them moving in for the handshake and you taking hold of their wrist, you have an opportunity to measure the amount of energy that they are injecting into the exercise. If you sense the slightest element of resistance, you may not get much further than moving their hand in front of their face. However, if you are able to sense a significant burst of energy, it is a natural and easy thing to move that hand up and over their head.

The key is not to fight against them or move their hand in unnatural ways. Instead, you accept their energy and employ only the slightest amount of redirection as you allow the energy to keep flowing (usually in a circular direction).

This is a difficult process to describe in words alone. However, an exercise may help to convey the kind of feeling you are looking for. Stand up and allow your hand to swing at your side a couple of times. Then allow it to swing behind you further, so that it swings further in front of you in an upwards direction. Then, allow it to swing behind you slightly more. This time, the hand will likely swing in front of you so much that the back of your hand almost touches your forehead.

Repeat this one more time. However, just as your hand is swinging in front of your face, use your other hand to apply the slightest touch to the back of the swinging hand, in line with the little finger. You will likely find your hand twisting and end up with your palm in front of your face.

This is a simple exercise to demonstrate how easy it is to apply the smallest amount of effort to redirect the energy of a moving hand. As you practice this, you may find that it is actually easier to end up with their hand above their head, than it is in front of their face. To an onlooker, it looks as if you have controlled the hand more. In reality, you have simply allowed the energy that they put into the handshake to flow further.

This exercise is one reason that we now teach people that the handshake does not need to be interrupted at the usual point. Instead, you can allow the hands to meet and after the hands have dropped slightly – as they do on most handshakes – when they are rising up again, you intervene and take hold of the hand. In this way, you respect the energy that your partner is putting into the upwards handshake and simply redirect it.

Once their hand is in front of their face, their fingertips at least level with their hair-line, if not higher, you can continue with patter like:

> "And as, and only as, that hand continues to move further towards your face, you can allow yourself to fall deeper into this experience...

"Yet, you will not fall deeply into trance until you feel your hand touching your face..."

Personally, I use the terminology of "falling" only inasmuch as it relates to their internal experience. I do not want to highlight the natural physiological fall of their hands.

Once their hand touches their face, you can congratulate them and imply that they are now in hypnosis. However, you may also then proceed to use some of the deepeners from the last chapter to intensify the experience.

## Moving their Hand Towards their Face

I talked in the last chapter about two means of ensuring your partner's hand moves towards their face. That is less of an issue with this variation, as hand placement almost guarantees an eventual move. However, there is a third means of moving their hands towards their face, which it is useful to know about, for this version and the previous.

This means of achieving hand movement also involves moving it for them, but in a slightly different way. After you have pointed at their hand and told them to look at it, you might continue as so:

"Just look at that hand and become aware of your eyes..."

[This is said whilst you are moving their hand centimetres closer and then further away from their face. The phrase 'become aware of your eyes' is intentionally vague.]

"That's it... And as you focus on that hand, resting your eyes on one spot..."

[You let go of the hand now, but at the exact moment that you have begun to move it forward, so there is still some minimal forward momentum.]

"Notice as that hand begins to want to move towards you..."

[You will most likely now only have your forefinger on the back of their hand, or no contact at all.]

"That's it... And as that hand moves towards your face...

"You can notice the changing focus of your eyes and note the tendency for your eyes to close..."

And so on!

## Which One and Why?

If you are wondering about the difference between this version ("falling hand") and the previous one ("floating hand"), it all comes down to the position of your partner's hand once the interrupted handshake has stopped. If their hand is effectively above their face, or feels heavy as if it will fall directly down easily, you would be more likely to go for the version in this chapter. (If it feels too heavy, you might skip falling to the face and let it fall to their side.) If their hand feels light in your hand, or ends with the finger-tips less than level with their eyes, then aim for floating hand, or frozen hand.

Think of it as a flowchart with the following questions:[3]

1) Where is their hand after the interrupt?

a) Above their head
b) Level with their eyes/nose
c) Below their nose

2) Is their hand heavy?

a) Yes
b) No

3) Are you trying to impress someone (and have plenty of Expectation to utilise)?

If 1a) then you will probably want to go for one variation or other of falling hand. If it feels heavy (2a), immediately go for a falling hand. If it feels light (2b), you could start with a frozen hand.
If 1b) and their hand is heavy, go for a falling hand deepener. Alternatively, you could hold their arm up under

---

3   We have provided a quick sketch of our flowchart in Appendix D. However, it is recommended that after you have experimented with the Bandler handshake, that you design one that more suits your needs and approach.

the elbow with your other hand, as you go for a focused hand. If their hand is light, go for a floating hand-to-face, or frozen hand.

If 1c) and their hand is heavy, you could either go straight to a falling hand deepener, or hold their arm up – until they take over – and go for a focused hand. If their hand is light, go for a frozen hand.

If the answer to 3) is "Yes," why not give the fast hand variation a go?

Rather than complicate matters, hopefully, that demonstrates the flexibility that this induction provides you with, if you follow your partner's lead. Of course, as you do that, you are always giving the impression that *they* are following *you*!

# GRAHAM OLD

# EXERCISE

Practice interrupting handshakes. Do this with a partner who knows what your overall aim is. However, each handshake you perform will be one of the following, with them not knowing in advance:

1. A normal handshake

2. An interrupted handshake, with you taking hold of their wrist just before your hands meet

3. An interrupted handshake, whereby your hands meet, drop down once and then just as the hands are moving up for another shake you take hold of their wrist and move their hand up in front of their face

4. An interrupted handshake, with you using as little energy as possible to see the highest position you can get their hand to finish at.

GRAHAM OLD

# The Frozen Hand

Interestingly, this is actually the original variation of the handshake, as taught by Bandler. He was less focused on the hand moving towards the face and more on the hand being momentarily cataleptic, before slowly floating down.

Nevertheless, you will find examples of Bandler employing the practice of moving his partner's hand closer and further away from their face, to cause mild confusion as they seek to focus. That can then be transformed into a floating hand-to-face, or a falling hand as below.

This variation effectively employs hand catalepsy, along with an eventual falling hand. However, the falling is down to your partner's side, not their face. It may not look as impressive to onlookers, but can be just as powerful an experience to those involved.

A simple transcript is enough to explain this variation.

[Hypnotist offers out their hand, as they say...]

"Thanks for coming along today."

[Their partner puts their hand out to shake hands. A split second before their hands meet, the hypnotist takes a hold of his partner's wrist with his other hand. He then swings the arm up in from of his partner's face.]

"Look at your hand..."

[Said whilst pointing at the hand that originally went in for the hand-shake.]

"And rest your eyes on one spot on that hand..."

[The hypnotist is employing tiny movements, invisible to onlookers, as he moves the hand slightly up and down, backwards and forwards for a few seconds.]

"Look at your hand, focus on your hand, and as you become aware of your eyes...

[Hypnotist blinks]

"... and the changing focus of your eyes

[Hypnotist blinks]

"...they can close now

[Hypnotist's pointing hand moves down]

"as you allow yourself to drop down inside and go to a deep place of peace..."

[Hypnotist lets go of hand if confident it will stay up.]

"...a place of comfort and relaxation."

"And you can find that you will drift deeply into that place, only as quickly as that hand comes down to a resting position at your side..."

[Hypnotist lets go of hand if they have not already done so.]

There is really not a lot more to it than that. As stated above, you may start by slowing moving your partner's hand closer or further from their face. These ambiguous movements create mild confusion and an uncertainty about where the hand is actually meant to be.

This uncertainty assists you, as once the hand rests, your partner is going to have an internal desire for the hand to stay where it is.

# GRAHAM OLD

# EXERCISE

Practice using the frozen hand variation of the Bandler handshake. You will see that continued practice results in natural and easy-flowing fluency, which is key!

Research the kind of words that you might want to use, as your partner's hand is frozen and then falling. It is common to speak about discovering resources. You might also want to use ambiguous language about e.g 'learning things that you already knew, but did not yet know that you knew.' You get the idea!

It can be helpful to play around with words that sound 'hypnotic' or 'trancey.' For example:

| | |
|---|---|
| Calm | Insights |
| Serene | Revelations |
| Peace | Space |
| Learnings | Time |
| Comfort | Connections |
| Journey | Present |
| Stillness | Resourceful |

# GRAHAM OLD

# The Focused Hand

This is the version we were taught by Jonathan Chase. It has a number of advantages to it:

1. It does not depend upon the subterfuge of interrupting a handshake

2. It can move into either a floating hand-to-face, or a frozen/falling hand-to-their-side.

Simply begin by asking, "are you left-handed or right-handed?" The answer they give is irrelevant, but they will assume that it means something. This adds to their tendency to project competency onto you.

Regardless of their answer, point to one of their hands and say, "Can I borrow that hand?" When they say, "yes" - which they will – lift the hand up so that they are facing their palm, about 12 inches from their face.

This variation works well if executed in a direct manner. So, it may proceed with clear directions as follows:

"Look at that hand.

"Focus on a shape in that hand.

"What shape is the shape?"

[Say this with complete congruency. They will not think that it is a strange question, unless you give them cause to do so.]

"What colour is that {shape}?"

[They answer.]

"Go into the {shape}.

"Go right into the {shape}."

[Their eyes may close at this point.]

"That's right.

"Just go right into the {shape}."

[If their eyes are not yet closed, you might say, something like this instead:]

"Just close your eyes as you go right into that {shape}.

"That's right.

"Keep going into that {shape} and lose yourself in that shape.

"And on the other side, you can find a place of complete calm and comfort, safety and serenity. This is a place of peace and relaxation, where you are free to be you and discover all of the resources at your disposal.

# THE HYPNOTIC HANDSHAKES

"And you can find that you will drift deeply into that experience, only as quickly as that hand comes down to a resting position at your side..."

# GRAHAM OLD

# **EXERCISE**

Use the focused hand variation on yourself, to get some idea of what it feels like.

Continue to practice your use of hypnotic language and "trancey" words. The idea is not to trick your partner, but to provide them with words that have ambiguous or incomplete meaning. They can then inject their own truth or experience into the words.

Next, practice the focused hand variation with a partner. This will likely be the least scary version to use for new hypnotists, as it is in effect little more than a direct and accelerated eye-fixation induction.

Continue to practice this variation with partners, asking them for feedback on their experience. However, you are not asking them to grade you. You are seeking to learn from their experience, as it may well be completely different to someone else that you practice with.

# GRAHAM OLD

# The Fast Hand

Derren Brown, the British mentalist and illusionist, is known for using what we originally called "the flashy hand" variation of the Bandler Handshake. This is the most direct and rapid of the variations. As such, there is not a great deal for us to describe!

[Go in for a handshake. As your partner's hand moves in for the shake, remove yours and take hold of their wrist with your other hand.]

[Move their hand up in front of their face.]

[As you move their hand closer to their face, say...]

Hypnotist: "Look at your hand, let your eyes close..."

[Move the hand forward until it is centimetres from their face. Then simultaneously have your other hand on the back of their neck and lightly but purposefully tap their head forward, as you touch their hand with their face and say...]

H: "Sleep!

"And just start to relax and sink all the way down.

"Right the way deep and right the way sound asleep."

You may then want to proceed with the deepeners included previously, where you lift up their arms and drop them by their sides.

This induction completely relies upon expectancy, with a slight element of expectant waiting that a pattern-interrupt brings.

There is a reason why Derren Brown gets away with this, when many of the rest of us would not. His audiences already expect strange and unusual behaviours from him – and they already presume that they may be putty in his hands. Thus, when he does something strange like pushing someone's hand against their face, they simply presume, "This must be when the magic starts!"

# **EXERCISE**

With a practice partner, experiment with the various versions of the Bandler Handshake you have been taught.

Does any particular version feel more natural to you?

Is there any version that you think you would be unlikely to use?

# GRAHAM OLD

# Pattern Interrupts

The Bandler Handshake induction falls under the category of "pattern interrupts." These are based on the idea that there are specific patterns of behaviour that our minds run outside of our conscious awareness as programs or strategies. These patterns will vary from culture to culture.

Every person, in fact every sub-culture, will have developed their own patterns - tasks that run on auto-pilot. Obvious examples would include a handshake (whereby, in many cultures, if you stick out your hand to someone, they will extend their hand to shake it with hardly a second thought), a verbal greeting routine ("Hi, how are you?" generating the response, "Fine, thanks. How are you?"), high-fives, waving, expressions of manners ("please," "thank-you," "you're welcome," "bless you," "have a nice day!") and so on.

If you interrupt one of these patterns with unexpected stimuli then your partner in the pattern becomes temporarily confused. They then have to briefly pause to consider which course to take. Think of it in this way: you explain the rules of a game to someone and then you begin to play the game. Five minutes in, you – as the more knowledgeable player – do something that appears to break the rules. For a split-second, your partner will look to you for an explanation.

I am not talking about those times when they say, "Hey, you can't do that!" I am referring to the split-second before they even consciously object. For a brief moment, you have paused their understanding of how things operate and they will be searching around for an explanation, or new direction.

We could describe this brief moment as expectant waiting. If you can justify why you played an apparently illegal or innovative move, you may just be able to carry on with the game smoothly and without objection. They are looking to you for an explanation, even if they are not aware of it. However, if you take too long, they will come to their own conclusion, evaluate the previously offered rules and conclude that you are cheating.

Obviously, all of this happens in the blink of an eye and eventually the "conscious mind" takes control again. However, for a split second, you have an opening, an opportunity to hi-jack the confusion and provide the direction for which they are subconsciously looking.

Simply put, for a brief second, they are looking at you and saying, "Hey, what gives?!" before that thought even consciously enters their mind.


## Re-direction, Not Obstruction

In 1980, Donald Saposnek wrote an article entitled, *Aikido: A Model for Brief Strategic Therapy*.[4] He was

---

4 Saposnek, D.T, 'Aikido: A Model for Brief Strategic Therapy.' In: Strozzi-Heckler, Richard. (1985). *Aikido And The New Warrior*. Berkeley, Calif.: North Atlantic Books.

building on the work of Watzlawick, who had noted some similarities between Judo and brief strategic therapy. Saposnek suggests that Aikido may be a more accurate model with which to make comparisons.

Aikido is a predominantly non-attacking Japanese martial art, based on the principles of harmony and the peaceful resolution of conflict. Similar to Judo (with which it shares a common root), a practitioner of aikido relies upon their attacker's energy to perform their defence. However, Saposnek notes that whilst Judo might be described by the adage, "Push when pulled, pull when pushed," aikido is more properly expressed as "Turn when pushed, and enter when pulled." The movement is a circular one, as the aikidoist *blends* with his partner's energy.

In fact, watching an experienced aikidoist at work, echoes the title of Terry Dobson's book on the subject: *It's a Lot Like Dancing.*[5] The blending of forces makes it almost impossible at times to see who is leading and who is following. The aikidoist does not confront or clash with their challenger. Instead, they accept and join the flow of their attacker's energy. In this way, the attacker has little opportunity for resistance, as nothing is offered to resist.

Once the aikidoist has *blended* with their partner's energy, they follow the movement to its natural end. Only at that point, do they *extend* the end point of the manoeuvre slightly further than it would naturally reach, causing their partner to be easily redirected. As someone who studied aikido for a number of years, I can vouch that it is not an uncommon experience to step forward to

5 Dobson, Terry, and Riki Moss. (1993). *It's a Lot like Dancing: An Aikido Journey.* Berkeley, CA: Frog.

attack your partner, only seconds later to find yourself on the floor, perhaps in an arm-lock, thinking, "How on earth did I get here?!"

Some of the parallels between aikido and hypnosis or hypnotherapy will no doubt be obvious. However, I am particularly interested in offering it as an example for performing pattern interrupts. If our partner experiences them as too direct, like a clash of different intentions, then we will most likely face resistance. Yet, if we can blend with our partner's energy (that is, the momentum behind the beginning of their pattern), we can more successfully redirect it, creating a whole new movement.

## Pattern Interrupts Beyond the Induction

The previous discussion has already introduced the idea that pattern interrupts can be used for more than inductions. They are actually an effective tool in therapy, self-help and almost any kind of human interaction.

The common example given for a pattern to interrupt is a handshake. Of course, this makes sense in cultures where a handshake is a natural social action. However, there is far more that can be interrupted.

Any kind of socially expected (and therefore ingrained) behaviour is a pattern that can be interrupted. A high-five, saying "bless you" to a sneeze, someone returning a smile and so on. In established relationships, you may have witnessed couples where one says, "I love you" and the other replies, "I love you too," without an ounce of affection in their voice! It was an habitual and automatic response.[6]

---

6   That does not mean, of course, that it was not real or genuine!

Stories are an example of a pattern that can be created and then interrupted. For starters, it is the case that most fictional stories follow very similar types of flow and structure. Adding in new directions, diversions or unexpected detours can cause an experience of excitement, expectancy or confusion in the reader's mind. However, even in therapy, stories can be used and interrupted effectively.

Nested loops can be thought of as stories within a story, though they can be as small as metaphors within a metaphor or even ideas within an idea. An example could be starting to tell a story with a familiar feel to it, perhaps it has a Little Red Riding Hood vibe, meaning your partner can fairly accurately predict where you are going. Then, at an unexpected point, you veer off into another story. For example, you might say something like:

> "My own grandmother once told me about a time when *she* was a little girl..."

Or:

> "I actually knew a wood-cutter once. He would always sing this song about..."

You have successfully taken the energy from the pattern (i.e. the familiarity of the plot), blended with it and redirected it.

In this example, we are now talking about when my grandmother was a little girl and I could perhaps talk about some lesson she learned or some antics she got up to with her best friend Eleanor. At that point, I would interrupt again, perhaps even during mid sentence, with a new direction, which this time contains a direct suggestion:

> "Eleanor Roosevelt once said, *Do one thing every day that scares you.*"

I would then go back to finish the story about my grandmother. When that "loop" was completed, I would finish the telling of my Red Riding Hood-esque tale. Structurally, this might look something like:

- Begin Story 1
  - Begin Story 2
    - Story 3 / Suggestions
  - End Story 2
- End Story 1

If your redirection at the point of Story 3, or the suggestion, is effective enough it will create a massive sense of confusion and/or expectancy from them. Additionally, for many people, this creates automatic amnesia for the suggestion, which may or may not be a desired result.

Other examples of pattern interrupts in a therapeutic setting would involve your very demeanour. If people are expecting you to be overly serious, yet you project a sense of light-heartedness, it can create all sorts of confusion. You might invite someone to sit in a chair, yet as their knees are bending, you could then say, "Oh, not that one. That's for when you go into hypnosis in a bit." Then invite them to sit in an alternate chair and say something like, "Let's decide how we are going to work together first." Obviously, you have given a suggestion that they will go into hypnosis later. Yet, also, by interrupting them mid-bend, you created a moment of anticipation whereby you can indirectly suggest how well the first part of your session might go.

One way that I like to interrupt patterns is by playing Devil's advocate. I always do this with a twinkle in my eye and most of the time, I forewarn people by saying something like:

> "I should just let you know that one successful client once described my style of therapy as being 'playfully provocative.' So, if at any point, you think I'm being rude or idiotic, just presume it's all part of the therapy and we'll get along just fine!"

This elicits a nod and a smile and on we go. However, it is amazing how often people do not take the warning seriously.

One woman came to my clinic to stop smoking. After I had given her my usual warning, I gathered as much information as I needed. When I asked her how many cigarettes she smoked a day, she laughed and said, "Oh, it's silly really. I only smoke 10 a day." As we carried on talking, I used the word "silly" a number of times, sometimes with a little chuckle in my voice as I did so.

After a while – and just before we were going to move into the magic hypnotic chair – she objected strongly, "It's not silly! It could kill..."

At that point, I slammed my hand on my desk and

said, "You're absolutely right! Sit in the other chair and let's stop this."

There were a number of pattern interrupts taking place for this woman, from me changing my style completely, interrupting her expectations, to literally interrupting her as she spoke. Working in this way can be somewhat like splashing a cup of cold water in someone's face if they are being hysterical. It creates a sudden shift in their awareness.

Pattern interrupts can help free people from Pavlovian responses. Yet, a pattern-interrupt is not always stopping the behaviour. It can be seen as redirecting it. In fact, when approached in this way it can face zero opposition, as your partner to some degree will still feel as if they are working on auto-pilot. It's just that you've reprogrammed that auto pilot!

As with the stories above, if it is felt helpful, all patterns can be finished as they usually would be. So, you might do the Bandler Handshake with someone, or the Ericksonian Ambiguous Touch taught later in this book. You then do your therapy or phenomena in the middle. And you finish by completing the handshake. Once again, as with the stories, this can often elicit automatic amnesia for what happens right at the deepest centre of the experience.

## Questioning The Pattern Interrupt

The only real problem with the notion of pattern-interrupts is that they can effect some people's confidence using inductions like the Bandler Handshake. It can seem as if you have a very small window during which you have a magical portal into someone's subconscious mind. Often, the idea is coupled with the notion that *any* suggestion given during that window of time will be automatically and unquestioningly accepted. So, the stakes are fairly high. And of course, you have to have the skill of an Aikido master to pull it off!

However, I would like to challenge that idea. I prefer to suggest that the idea of a pattern-interrupt is simply a convoluted way of saying 'act in an unexpected manner, causing someone to look to you for an explanation.' I do believe that if you act smoothly and quickly enough, someone may not even realise they are looking to you for directions, but that is still a far-cry from the usual quasi-magical notion of pattern-interrupts as taught by some people.

In effect, we are simply talking about someone looking at you and saying, "Er, what's going on?"

Some people have suggested that as the Bandler Handshake can be executed without the pattern-interrupt element (e.g *the focused hand* seen above), then it is clearly not the pattern-interrupt that makes it work. This seems like fairly shaky logic to me.

The fact that if I do A+B, then you will do C, does not mean that it is impossible to achieve C without B. Additionally, the fact that on occasions, I can do only A and you will do C, does not mean that when I do B it is unimportant. In reality, the pattern-interrupt version of the Bandler Handshake and the non-pattern-interrupt version are two different inductions that are effective for different reasons.

Nevertheless, if you are at all concerned about the timing/execution of a pattern-interrupt, it can be useful to start by becoming proficient with the Focused Hand variation. Once you are comfortable with that, it will most likely feel like a small step to begin incorporating pattern-interrupt variations.

# EXERCISE

Take some time to practice and notice patterns in people's behaviour. For example, you might fake a sneeze and notice how many people say, "Bless you," without even looking up. (These will vary from culture to culture.)

Can you think of patterns which, if interrupted, would provide you with a brief window of expectant waiting?

Do you think that the focused-hand variation of the Bandler handshake means that the idea of pattern-interrupts is irrelevant and misleading?

Continue practising the Bandler handshake. Get used to the flexibility that comes from not knowing what version you are going to use first.

# GRAHAM OLD

# The Elman Handshake

Dave Elman originally referred to this as the 'catalyst induction.' However, it did not always involve a handshake. In fact, in his classic book *Hypnotherapy*, Elman teaches this induction via three puffs on a cigarette!

The induction itself can be explained fairly easily:

- Tell your partner to look you in the eyes.

- Tell them that you will shake their hand three times.

- Explain that on the first shake, "you can allow yourself to relax. You know what it feels like to really let go. Want that and you can have it."

- Explain that on the second shake, "you will relax so much, that your eyes will want to close, but fight it. Don't let them close just yet."

- Then say that, on the third shake, "you can close your eyes and let go completely as you go inside."

- Take their hand and explain again what will happen with the first shake. Shake their hand 2 or 3 times. Let go of the hand.

- Take their hand again and explain what will happen with the second shake. Shake their hand 2 or 3 times. Let go of their hand.

- Take their hand a third time and explain again what will happen with this shake. Lift their hand up as you begin a hand-shake. However, as the hand is coming down, tug it down and forward slightly as you say something like, "Sleep..." or "Close your eyes and go inside."[7]

## Notes on Delivery

You may have noticed, that as the handshake is being pre-explained, it is unclear if the client is being told what will happen, or instructed as to what to do. This is intentional. The second time that events are explained, just before the handshake, you may want to be more direct and make it clear that you are making a direct suggestion as to what will happen.

Your own style and preferences will dictate how you word things – and how you want your partner to experience them. However, we have found this ambiguity to be useful.

---

7  This is not the kind of yank or jerking movement you might see used by a Stage Hypnotist. Instead, you are simply drawing them forward and down, causing their head to naturally and smoothly fall forward. A sudden jolt is far from necessary.

# THE HYPNOTIC HANDSHAKES

Reg Blackwood teaches a nice element to this handshake.[8] He suggests, during the first two handshakes, saying, "fight it" when or if you see nothing happening. This then encourages them to produce the phenomena they are told to fight against. Secondly, he says, "That's it," when their eyelids flicker, or begin to close.

I tend to say "that's it" even if all they do is blink. However, you can also simply nod your head as they blink.

Some people who use this induction, do not have their partner look them in the eyes. Instead, they ask them to look at the cheek bone just below their eyes. Or, they instruct them to look at their earlobe. Both of these options result in a situation where the subject feels that someone is looking into their eyes, yet although they are very close to returning the gaze, they are not quite there. This is a powerful if disconcerting experience, which simply serves to confirm that something unusual is happening.

If you do ask your partner to look into your eyes, I recommend practising your hypnotic gaze. I like to have my left eye focusing just in front of their eyeball, whilst my right eye looks through their eye to the back of their skull. This will give a defocused effect and will cause your partner to be unsure whether you are looking at them or not. However, this is not an essential element, as long as your hypnotic gaze conveys authority, assurance and expectation.

The tug on the third shake is not necessary, if that is

---

8 In fact, if you are looking for examples of this induction online, it is Reg's videos we would recommend.

not your preferred way of working. It does, however, add an additional element to the induction. Even if you do choose to employ it, you can be shaking their hand the third time until you see their eyes close. At that point, it is natural to have some kind of climatic action to confirm that they are now in hypnosis. So, a gentle pull down as the hand is naturally coming down from a shake will be more than enough.

Finally, some people object to the word "sleep" being used, as hypnosis is not sleep. That is a natural enough objection, but it is also one that is easily addressed. During all of my pre-talks, I talk about hypnosis being like going to the land of day-dreams, where all kinds of possibilities are within our reach. I emphasise that sometimes in a daydream we can still hear everything and everyone around us, but at other times, we are a million miles away, as if our teacher is calling out our name, but we are just too enveloped in bliss to pay it any attention. I then say that hypnosis is not the same as being asleep, but that I still *sometimes* use that word because it is a good signal to our brains to return to the land of day-dreams.

Feel free to steal my explanation, or simply say that hypnotic sleep is not sleep as we know it.

## The Principles at Work

There are a few principles that make this induction work. Firstly, you tell your partner to fight certain experiences. To do this effectively involves them 'locating' those experiences. This is akin to the 'do not think of a pink elephant' exercise you no doubt know of. However, in this instance, you are saying to them, "When I shake your hand, whatever you do, you have to make absolutely sure that you do not think of a pink elephant." You are actually inviting them to put extra effort into the activity that will bring about the very thing they are avoiding.

Secondly, you utilise your partner's responses, acting as if each one is exactly what they were supposed to do. They will naturally blink at some point and you will acknowledge it as them fighting the urge to close their eyes. They will exhale and you can welcome it as a sign that they are relaxing. Then, finally, their head will come slightly forward on the final shake as you direct them, "That's right, all the way down..."

Thirdly, the predominant principle that this induction relies upon is the element of expectation. We will explore that further in the next chapter. Suffice it to say for now, that as each shake produces the results you said, expectation is increased that the following shake will be equally effective.

## The Elman Handshake in Practice

The following transcript of the Elman Handshake being used demonstrates that there are no hard and fast rules as to what outcome is attached to which handshake. For example, above we described stating that your partner will simply relax on the first shake. Yet, in the following transcript, the hypnotist mentions the eyes wanting to close on the very first shake. The only advice we would give is that each handshake includes the previous phenomena and then takes it forward to the next stage. So, if you feel like you can generate enough expectancy that you can go for heavy eyes on the first handshake, there is no reason not to go for it.

Speak confidently, act congruently and your partner will follow your lead.

Hypnotist: "Just take my hand, and look into my eyes. That's it. Fix your eyes there."

[The following instructions are given whilst the hypnotist holds their partner's hand.]

H: "Here's what is going to happen: I am going to shake your hand 3 times. The first time I shake your hand, you're going to relax so much that your eyes are gonna start to feel tired. They are going to get quite heavy. You know the feeling when you're reading a book late at night and you're struggling to keep them open?"

Partner: "Yeah."

H: "That's going to happen the first time I shake your hand. But I want you to fight it and keep them open.

"The second time I shake your hand, there will be a really strong urge for your eyes to close, but I want you to try and fight it. If they do close...

[Partner blinks]

H: "That's right... I want you to try to open them again... until, the third time I shake your hand.

# THE HYPNOTIC HANDSHAKES

"And the third time I shake your hand, your eyes will close, your head will drop forward slightly and you will enter into that daydream place of hypnosis.

"Okay?"

P: "Yeah."

[Begins Handshakes. The hand is shaken continuously as the hypnotist repeats what will happen. That is, each "handshake" is actually a series of shakes. The hypnotist only stops shaking between the instructions]

H: "The first time I shake your hand now, your eyes are gonna start to feel tired, beginning to feel heavy..."

[Waits for a blink]

"That's right... But I want you to fight it and do your best to try and keep them open.

"The second time I shake your hand now, there will be a strong urge for your eyes to close, but I want you to fight it."

[Waits for a blink]

"That's right..."

[Partner slightly closes their eyes]

H: "But I want you to do your best to open them..."

[Partner opens their eyes, blinking repeatedly]

"That's right... try to keep them open.

"And now the third time I shake your hand, your eyes close, your head drops forward...

"...And sleep!"

[Hypnotist pulls hand further down and forward on the downward shake as they say, "Sleep."]

"That's right... relaxing all the way down. "

[Arm-drop deepener:]

"And as this arm just plops into your lap, you can go ten times as deep..."

[Hypnotist lets arm go]

"And as your other arm just falls by your side, you can go twice as deep into that experience..."

[Hypnotist picks up the other arm and just drops it into their lap.]

"All the way down... sinking, drifting, floating, deeper into that pleasant experience..."

# EXERCISE

Practice the Elman Handshake with a partner. Introduce it by suggesting that all they have to do is follow your instructions.

If you are more comfortable, re-word it such that it is your partner taking themselves into hypnosis. This removes any fear of failure, if confidence is an issue.

Alternatively, you might use the version where eye-closure is not mentioned until the second shake:

1st Shake: Relax
2nd Shake: Relax further and resist eye-closure
3rd Shake: Eyes close and go into hypnosis.

It may further help your confidence to start with a good pre-talk.[9] That way, you can be sure that your partner knows what going into hypnosis entails.

---

9   See http://www.howtodoinductions.com/pretalk

GRAHAM OLD

# Expectancy

The Elman handshake clearly relies upon one of the five core elements of effective inductions, discussed earlier: expectancy. As the psychologist, Irving Kirsch wrote, 'expectancy is an essential aspect of hypnosis, perhaps its most essential aspect.'[10]

The field of medicine has long recognised the power of the "placebo effect." This is a situation where a patient's belief that they are getting an active drug when they are only receiving a sugar pill can generate the same level of positive effect as if they had been given an actual drug.

Practically all approaches to psychotherapy emphasise the role of positive expectations in enhancing results. A commonly used term is 'self-fulfilling prophecies' - the recognition that our behaviour can adjust to match our expectations, thereby increasing the likelihood of their fulfilment.

If you think of many of the practices of a typical hypnotherapist, creating expectancy is the desired goal of almost all of them. It starts with dressing smartly, to convey professionalism. Next comes hanging Certificates on the wall to announce your credibility. Similarly, you might have business cards with C.Ht. after your name.

10 Kirsch, I. (1990). *Changing Expectations: A key to effective psychotherapy.* Pacific Grove, CA: Brooks/Cole, p. 143.

There's a good chance that your office would be connected in some way with a medical or health centre, to demonstrate the respectability and validity of hypnosis.

Then, think of some of the hypnotic rituals aimed at building positive expectations in the client. Some of what are termed 'suggestibility tests' are not solely to provide the hypnotist with information regarding a client's susceptibility to hypnosis. Instead, they are intended to convince the 'subject' that they are hypnotisable, or perhaps even already in hypnosis.

Hypnotic phenomena may also be used throughout a hypnotherapy session, both to maintain the expectancy, but also to increase it. So, if a client becomes aware that their arm is floating up into the air, whilst they sit there like an innocent observer, they will receive compelling evidence that they are in hypnosis. They will also have their expectations of the hypnotherapist confirmed and continue to believe that they can and will respond to his or her suggestions.

It is within the context of discussing how hypnotherapists aim to create expectancy, that Michael Yapko writes, 'Suffice it to say that helping clients to co-create a compelling vision of what's possible in their lives is one of the most important things that can happen in therapy.'[11] It seems fair to suggest that such a vision starts with what is possible in and through the hypnosis session itself.

---

11  Yapko, M. (2003). *Trancework: An Introduction to the Practice of Clinical Hypnosis*. New York: Routledge, p.137.

## The Response-Expectancy Model

Irving Kirsch has described a model of hypnosis that he calls response-expectancy theory. We do not adhere to any one particular model of hypnosis, preferring a more experiential approach.[12] Nevertheless, as Kirsch's model heavily emphasises the role of expectancy in hypnosis, it may be beneficial for us to explore it further at this point.

Building upon the idea of the placebo effect, Kirsch provides significant evidence to demonstrate that much of the effect of hypnosis is due to positive expectations on the part of the client. He even goes so far as to describe hypnosis as 'non-deceptive placebo.'

According to Response-Expectancy Theory, 'when we expect a particular outcome we sometimes unwittingly behave so as to produce that outcome.'[13] Kirsch proposes that subjects in a hypnotic situation generally have the belief (that is, the 'response expectancy') that they will follow the hypnotist's instructions and will likely carry out behaviours that could be experienced as automatic or involuntary. The result is that these subjects attribute hypnotic responses to external causes (in this case, the hypnotist) and experience them as involuntary.

Hypnotic responses, according to this model, are carried out in precisely the same way as voluntary responses. The only difference is in how the behaviours are experienced and interpreted.

If we return to the idea of an arm levitation being used in hypnosis, either as a 'suggestibility test,' or hypnotic

---

12  See *The Anatomy of Inductions,* where we first discussed this idea.

13  Michael, Garry & Kirsch, (2012). 'Suggestion, Cognition and Behavior.' In: *Current Directions in Psychological Science 2*, p.153.

phenomena during a session, it is easy to see the type of experience that Kirsch is referring to. Yet, whether you agree with Kirsch's model or not, it is difficult to dismiss it completely. It is beyond doubt that expectancy is a core component in the hypnotic experience.

## Expect More

John Cleesattel has a model of hypnosis which is markedly different to Kirsch's. Nevertheless, expectancy plays a key part in his model too, as the following quote demonstrates:

> 'When we expect something to happen, when we anticipate an outcome, our Imagination automatically reacts to it and prepares us for the expected event. ...Our Imagination treats it as an impending reality, then starts adapting our body to cope with the reality of it, and then just waits for the start of the anticipated event.'[14]

Cleesattel is making the significant point that not only does our imagination consider that something is about to happen, but it actually prepares for it. If this is the case, we can see why Kirsch would argue that expectancy is the most essential aspect of hypnosis.

This may be why many hypnotists begin a session with 'easier' phenomena, before working their way up to something considered more difficult. The idea is that it is

---

14  See http://www.wizardoftrance.com/expectancy

perhaps a simple task for a client to expect their eyes to close, as they feel more relaxed. Once this is achieved, it is easy for them to expect that their eyes will stay shut when you make that suggestion, and so on. For some people, this type of staggered approach is completely unnecessary. They are comfortable with the expectation that they will do whatever you tell them to do. However, for many people, it does appear to be helpful.

An extension of this, which is widely used, but not often admitted, is to start with naturally occurring phenomena. Some hypnotists start their sessions or routines with the exercise known as magnetic fingers.[15] Yet, that phenomena has absolutely nothing to do with hypnosis – *unless you say it has*! It works on purely physiological grounds, which is what makes it perfect as an opening gambit. It requires no level of expectation from your client and will work unless there is intentional resistance or a physical difficulty of some kind. Once the phenomena has been achieved, your client will usually then have at least some expectancy that they will experience what you next tell them they will.

Similarly, if I ask you to sit in my comfortable chair and speak to you with a soft and soothing voice, asking you to "rest" your eyes on a fixed spot above your eye-line, when I make the suggestion that your eyes will get heavy, it is a simple thing for you to expect that to happen. That is a very good place to start building a compelling vision of how things could be.

In the appendices, I have included John Cleesattel's version of an Expectancy Induction. It works precisely along the lines of his quote above, with the body

---

15  http://howtodoinductions.com/exercises/fingers

preparing to experience what you say it will, thereby ensuring that it does. A similar line of thought went through my head when someone at a party, who knew I was a hypnotist, asked me to do "some quick Derren Brown stuff." I have transcribed this below to demonstrate that expectancy is an incredibly natural thing, but can produce powerful experiences for those we utilise it for.

## An Impromptu Hypnosis/Mentalism Routine

Hypnotist: "In a moment you will think a new thought. Nod your head when you do."

[Partner nods their head]

H: "Say it out-loud."

P: "I feel silly!" [Laughs]

H: "No, I said you will have a *new* thought. You've thought that old thing plenty of times!"

P: [Laughs then nods head]

H: "Okay, if you can, say it out-loud."

P: "I can do this..."

H: "Excellent. Now, in a moment, you will find your *body* thinking, 'I want to relax.' Let me know when it does... and then let it do so."

P: [Nods head]

# THE HYPNOTIC HANDSHAKES

H: "Okay, So, you can go ahead and *let it relax*."

P: [Shoulders drop and they blink for longer than usual]

H: "In a moment, I am going to put a thought into your head. And the thought that will enter your head is, 'I am so relaxed, I want to close my eyes...' And when that happens, you can go ahead and let them close."

P: [Closes Eyes]

H: "Now, in a moment, not yet but in a moment, the following thought will enter your head, 'I am *so* relaxed, I cannot open my eyes.' *Want that* and you can have it. And when that happens, you will drift even deeper into that relaxation. And when you've done that, nod your head, to let me know you've had that thought..."

P: [Nods head]

H: "Now, to demonstrate the power of your subconscious mind in achieving that relaxation for you, go ahead and try to open those relaxed eyes, finding that the more you try the more relaxed they become..."

P: [Raises eyebrows a number of times, attempting to open their eyes, but eventually gives up and laughs...]

H: "In a moment, I am going to put one more thought into your head. And the thought that will enter your head is, 'I can open my eyes whenever I want.' And the second you think that, not yet, your eyes will automatically pop open, leaving you feeling so great, you'll want to fetch me a Beer to thank me..."

P: [Laughs]

H: "So, get ready. When I am putting that thought into your head, I will say the word 'now' and when I do so, your eyes will pop open, you will feel incredible and you will get me that beer.

"Ready?"

P: "Yeah."

H: "I am putting... that thought... into your head... ...NOW!"

P: [Eyes open fully. He blinks a number of times, laughs and claps.]

P: "Fancy a beer?!"

# EXERCISE

Practice the Elman Handshake (or, 'the catalyst induction') with things other than a handshake.

- Clapping your hands
- Blinking (you or them!)
- Tapping their knee
- Coughing...

The options are practically limitless!

# GRAHAM OLD

# The Erickson Handshake

Erickson's 'ambiguous touch' handshake is undoubtedly the source of Bandler's Handshake. Yet, it is often rejected in favour of the latter. One reason it is neglected appears to be that people see how simple it is, presume that there must be something more taking place 'under the surface' and therefore conclude that the ambiguous touch is too difficult for them.

It is both accurate and misleading to describe Erickson's handshake as either simple or difficult. I would prefer to suggest that it is simple *and* complex. On the surface, it can be as easy to execute as it appears. However, there is no doubt that there are deeper processes and principles at work which ensure that the induction will prove effective.

This chapter will take a slightly different direction to the previous ones in this book. We will mainly concentrate on sharing various transcripts of the induction in practice, each performed in a slightly different way, with very little discussion. Then, in the next chapter, we will unpack the principle of *Kinaesthetic Confusion*.

## Hypnotic Realities

The following transcript is taken from Erickson's own

discussion of his induction, in *Hypnotic Realities*.[16]

> E: "Now silently, mentally, count backwards from 20 to 1.
>
> "You can begin the count, now."
>
> [Erickson shakes hands with S but lingers before releasing her hand. Gradually, and with seeming hesitation, he alternately applies and releases pressure with his fingers on different parts of her hand. S is not even sure when he finally disengages his hand. Her hand is left in a cataleptic position in midair. During this handshake Erickson looks toward her face but focuses on the wall behind her. She looks at his face and seemingly tries to capture his gaze or note whether or not he is actually looking at her. She seems a bit disconcerted by his faraway gaze.]
>
> E: "Do you think you're awake? [Said without altering his faraway gaze past her.]"
>
> S: "I never really know." [laughs]
>
> S: "I am. I guess... I'm foggy."

Erickson continues to utilise this open-eyed trance, along with conversationally achieving hallucinations, age regression, time distortion and amnesia.

The thing that is notable about this example is that

---

16 Erickson & Rossi, *Hypnotic Realities*, p. 84.

THE HYPNOTIC HANDSHAKES

Erickson gives his client something to do mentally whilst he is ambiguously touching/releasing her hand. This dual focus is one that we recommend, but is not always necessary.

## Pantomime Induction

On one occasion, Erickson was lecturing on hypnosis in South America. Not being fluent in Spanish, he employed a non-verbal induction. Erickson's description of how he presented the handshake induction follows:[17]

'She was brought through a side door to confront me. Silently we looked at each other, and then, as I had done many times previously with seminarians in the United States in seeking out what I consider clinically to be "good responsive" subjects before the beginning of the seminar and hence before I was known to them, I walked towards her briskly and smilingly and extended my right hand and she extended hers. Slowly I shook hands with her, staring her fully in the eyes even as she was doing to me and slowly I ceased smiling. As I let loose of her hand, I did so in a certain irregular fashion, slowly withdrawing it, now increasing the pressure slightly with my thumb, then with the little finger, then with the middle finger, always in an uncertain irregular, hesitant manner and finally so gently withdrawing my hand that she would have no clearcut

17 Erickson, M.H. 'Pantomime techniques in hypnosis and the implications.' *American Journal of Clinical Hypnosis*, 1964, 7, pp. 64-70. Quoted in Gilligan, p.252.

awareness of just when I had released her hand or what part of her hand I had last touched. At the same time, I slowly changed the focus of my eyes by altering their convergence, thereby giving her a minimal but appreciable cue that I seemed to be looking not at but through her eyes and off into the distance.

'Slowly, the pupils of her eyes dilated, and as they did so, I gently released her hand completely, leaving it in mid-air in a cataleptic position. A slight upward pressure on the heel of her hand raised slightly. Then catalepsy was demonstrated in the other arm also and she remained staring unblinkingly... Slowly I closed my eyes and so did she.'

This induction is initiated by approaching someone to shake hands. The handshake takes place and the induction begins as the hands are being loosened. The loosening transitions from a:

'firm grip into a gentle touch by the thumb, a lingering drawing away of the little finger, a faint brushing of the subject's hand with the middle finger – just enough vague sensation to attract the attention. As the subject gives attention to the touch of your thumb, you shift to a touch with your little finger. As the subject's attention follows that, you shift to a touch with your middle finger and, then again, to the thumb. ...the withdrawal from the handshake is arrested by this attention arousal, which establishes a waiting set, an expectancy. ...touch the undersurface of the hand (wrist) so gently that it barely suggests an upward push. This is followed by a similar slight downward touch, and then, I sever contact so gently that the subject does not know exactly when – and the subject's hand is left going neither up nor down, but cataleptic. Sometimes I give a lateral and medial touch so that the hand is even more rigidly cataleptic.'[18]

## That's Right!

As with most versions of the Erickson Handshake, this induction involves engaging in the handshake. Then, the hands are released in a slow and ambiguous manner, which results in catalepsy.

[The hypnotist offers his hand for a shake, which is accepted. As he shakes hands, his other hand can be holding his partner's forearm or elbow.]

Hypnotist: "Just look in my eyes."

[The hypnotist maintains a gaze that looks through their partner's eyes, or stops just before reaching their eyes.]

[The handshake slows down.]

---

18 Erickson, M.H., and Ross, E.L. (1976). 'Two-level communication and the microdynamics of trance and suggestion.' American Journal of Clinical Hypnosis, 18, p. 108. Quoted in Battino, *Ericksonian Approaches*, p.233.

H: "That's right..."

[Each time their partner blinks or shows any 'minimal cues,' the hypnotist affirms this with a nod, or by saying, "that's right."[19]]

H: That's right..."

[The hypnotist slowly removes his hand from the handshake. Simultaneously, he lessons the support provided by his other hand. At times, this hand pushes up slightly, then lets the hand fall down a little, before continuing to support it. Eventually, the hand is removed completely.]

H: That's right..."

[The hypnotist is eventually supporting the arm merely with one finger, which he slowly removes.]

H: That's right... They can close..."

[The Falling Arm deepener (see below) is employed at this stage.]

## Overloading Confusion

Some of the transcripts in this chapter have used more than physical confusion. They have also introduced an

---

19 See *Mastering the Leisure Induction*, pp. 69-72, for discussion of minimal cues.

element of mental overload. This may simply be a matter of personal preference. However, although the *"That's Right"* and *Pantomime* versions may appear most impressive to onlookers, we tend to opt for versions that also contain a cognitive element. The following is one such example:

[The Hypnotist shakes hands with his partner.]

Hypnotist: "I'd like you to take some time to think about your earliest happy memory now...]

[As you observe eye-movements or other cues that suggest your partner has "gone inside," continue...]

H: "I do not want you to merely float back to your earliest memory, as interesting as that may be... Neither do I want you to go straight to your happiest memory, which I imagine would be a lot of fun, right?" [Waits for a sign of recognition...]

H: "Instead, I want you to go to your earliest happy memory."

[Pressure is subtly being shifted in the handshake. Touch is moved from the top of the hand to the bottom. The middle finger drags across the palm as the hand slowly proceeds to move out of the shake.]

H: "At the same time, you can go ahead and allow your favourite song to play in the background of that memory.

[The hand continues to be released slowly, perhaps with the other hand gently cupping the arm underneath, though this is not necessary.]

H: "I can only wonder how much joy it would bring those people who love you the most to relive this happy memory with you. Seeing what you see, hearing the sounds, feeling all of those positive sensations..."

H: "That's right..." [Said as/when their partner blinks or shows any minimal cues.]

H: "Feel their love deep inside. Feel their love in that arm there."

[The hand/arm is lifted slightly, then allowed to naturally fall back down. It is then moved imperceptibly to one side... and then back.]

H: "That's right. Enjoy that experience right now..." [Said as the hand/arm is completely released and left cataleptic.]

H: "As you marvel at how easily your powerful mind can recreate all of those sensations here and now..."

[The Falling Arm deepener (see below) is employed at this stage.]

There are other mental overloads that can be employed, to go alongside the ambiguous touches. Two that are sometimes recommended are:

1) Count backwards from 1000, in 3s. So, 1000, 997, 994, etc.

As my partner appears to be getting more 'entranced' in their experience, I may suggest that the numbers can just drift away, as they drift also deeper into trance.

2) Picture yourself drawing in the air a massive lower-case letter "a." Simultaneously, silently and mentally say the letter, "z." Then draw the second letter of the alphabet, whilst saying the second from last letter and so on.

Recently, I have enjoyed shaking hands whilst saying something like:

Hypnotist: "What I would like you to do in a moment, each time you breathe out, is to mentally spell out a month of the year backwards... one letter per exhalation. Let me give you an example:"

[Breathes out, whilst saying the letter...] "R... But, of course you'll be saying it in your head..."

[Breathes-in]

[Breathes out, whilst saying the letter...] "E"

[Breathes-in]

[Breathes out, whilst saying the letter...] "B"

"And so on. You understand."

[Partner nods]

H: "I would like you to start with December and work backwards. Is that okay with you?"

P: "Yeah."

H: "So, as you begin to do that now, you can wonder about the wonderful places you have been. And maybe your mind takes you to one whenever you feel the need to relax...."

"And I don't know where or when you go, but I do know that you can take yourself there whenever you please..."

[Lets go of hand]

"...Did you know you can do that?"

[The question is ambiguous, as they are unclear whether I am asking about their ability to take their mind off somewhere else, or their cataleptic arm.]

(One of the things I like about this particular mental distraction is that it affords the hypnotist all kinds of opportunities to play around with words related to time and space. And they are usually 'under' before they've even started spelling, certainly by the time I have let go

100

of their hand. I should note that after a while, I tell them that they can just let those months and letters fade away now, time floating off into space. It's a patter that I would recommend experimenting with at least once.)

You do not want to be too confusing as to simply annoy your partner. At the same time, you do not want to occupy their mind so much that they fail to go into trance, or ignore what is happening in their arm. This may sound like a tricky balance to get, but with practice you will find it coming naturally enough.

## The Falling Arm Deepener

We first encountered this deepener when looking at The Floating Hand. It is the most recommended means of proceeding only because it makes meaningful sense of what your partner is experiencing and provides a way to deepen their experience, with no extra work on your part!

At its most simple, the deepener may involve little more than:

> "And you won't *go all of the way into hypnosis* until that hand happens to gradually go all of the way down, completely... in its own time..."

A fuller example may look something like:

> "As that hand begins to gradually drift down in its own time, you can find yourself drifting deeper into that experience... And you may not have known that you have this ability to access that deep resourceful subconscious state of yours,

quite so easily... Yet, now that you have, you may see, or experience or simply know the solutions to all of those issues that have been troubling you. You may or may not yet know how to get there from here, but you will find yourself increasingly knowing exactly where it is that you want to go..."

Once the arm/hand has reached their side or lap, it is up to you whether you choose to continue intensifying their experience even further:

"And in a moment, I will take your arm and just drop it by your side, allowing you to go twice as deep..."

[Lift up their arm by the wrist. It should feel heavy, as if you are doing all of the lifting. If it does not, shake it slightly from side to side, as if you are relaxing it further. Then allow the arm to drop down.]

"And in a moment, I will take your [other] arm and just drop it by your side, finding yourself going deeper still, deeper, deeper, deepest...
all the way down..."

[Lift up their other arm by the wrist. Then allow the arm to drop down.]

"That's right..."

# EXERCISE

Practice the Erickson Handshake. When you are beginning to get used to this induction, it can help to have one hand under their forearm, or elbow, whilst the other hand is shaking theirs.

That may sound unnatural, but it is how some people shake hands anyway.

Practice the different variations discussed in this chapter:

- With simultaneous verbal overload
- Pantomime (non-verbal)
- That's Right

GRAHAM OLD

# Kinaesthetic Confusion

In his exceptional volume, *Therapeutic Trances*, Stephen Gilligan rightly notes that Confusion – when used as a hypnotic technique – predominantly relies upon the practices of *interruption* and *overload*.[20] Erickson's ambiguous touch handshake perfectly utilises both.

When he was faced with a client who was willing to go into trance, but struggled to set aside their conscious processes to do so, Erickson would often employ confusion. (Other techniques he relied upon at times included boredom, distraction and ideomotor dissociation.) However, whilst confusion is still recommended today as a means of hypnotising the so-called "analytical subjects," such an idea is not always expressed in the way that Erickson espoused it.

Personally, I have seen dozens of transcripts of inductions that were supposedly perfect for the apparently hard-to-hypnotise. On the whole, these were pre-written scripts of gobbledegook, presumably intended to make the client clueless as to what you are actually talking about. Such an approach understands a little of the purpose and power of confusion, but only a little.

In keeping with the subject of this book, we will focus predominantly on *kinaesthetic* confusion. However, I feel

---

20 See Gilligan, Stephen, *Therapeutic Trances*, p. 235.

that it is necessary to say a little more about these popular means of using confusion to induce hypnosis. Confusion is best employed for those clients who perhaps struggle to shut-off part of their conscious mind, or focus in on the specifics of what you are saying. This may be due to an autistic spectrum condition, ADHD, personality types, thinking styles or any other reason. That is all irrelevant. The one relevant thing is how you utilise their active mind.

It is precisely the utilisation of such a mind that many confusion inductions fail to do. Instead, as you read inductions for "analyticals," you may notice that they almost attempt to bombard the subject with confusion after confusion. Incomplete sentences, ambiguities, non sequiturs, grammatical or syntactical violations... these are fired at the client one after the other, as if the expected outcome is that their mind will eventually give way and say, "I surrender. Please command me."

This could not be further from Erickson's approach, who noted, 'One should bear in mind that these patients are highly motivated, that their disinterest, antagonism, belligerence, and disbelief are actually allies bringing about the eventual result.'[21] This suggests that rather than attempting to overcome a client's "over-active," "analytical" or "resistant" mind, the Ericksonian hypnotist would aim to utilise it as an ally. So it is that Gilligan concludes:

'Confusion techniques utilise whatever the client is doing to inhibit trance or other therapeutic

---

21 Rossi, E. L. (Ed.) *The collected papers of Milton H. Erickson, Volume 1: The nature of hypnosis and suggestions.* New York: Irvington. 1980, p. 286.

developments *as the basis for inducing those developments.*[22]

Confusion inductions typically rely upon the assumption that there are automatic behaviours or thoughts that each person tends towards. This, of course, fits with our discussion of pattern-interrupts above. Gilligan states that acceptance of this assumption is also based on the following:

1. Disruption of any of these patterns creates a state of uncertainty dominated by undifferentiated arousal (e.g. confusion)
2. Most people strongly dislike uncertainty states and are hence extremely motivated to avoid them
3. The arousal will increase unless the person can attribute it to something ("this happened because...")
4. As uncertainty increases, so does the motivation to reduce it
5. The person who is highly uncertain will typically accept the first viable way by which the uncertainty can be reduced (e.g. suggestions to drop into trance).

Of course, the first step in all of this is in recognising an individual's conditioned or patterned behaviours. This is where pre-written confusion scripts often fall down. Some people are perfectly happy with grammatical violations and completely unfazed by incomplete sentences. A better approach is to at least spend some

---

22  Gillian, Op cit. p. 236. Emphasis mine.

time calibrating a client's behaviour. This means developing an awareness of your client's usual way of being. For example, for many people, avoiding eye-contact can be a sign that they are hiding something. Yet, for some people with e.g. autism, it can simply be a natural way of engaging. If we approached people like cookie-cutter variations of each other and thereby attempted to 'confuse' them, we would completely miss the point of Erickson's utilisation.

Nevertheless, it is the case that in many societies, there are patterns that are so ingrained that they can be assumed, *unless evidence suggests otherwise*. So, if you go in for a handshake and your partner looks at you first, that may be a good indication that it is not a natural or patterned behaviour for them. However, in most cases, for those of us in the West at least, a handshake is still a reliably predictable pattern.

It is the fifth point of Gilligan's that needs expounding. Many new hypnotists or NLP practitioners act as if this is a magic doorway into someone's subconscious mind. This type of magical thinking does not do any one any favours. If you walk up to someone who has absolutely no awareness of hypnosis and for whom 'sleep' carries no metaphorical connotations, interrupting their handshake and then yelling, "Sleep!" will achieve little more than bemusement. As Gilligan points out, people are i) looking for something to attribute the interruption to and ii) seeking a *viable* way to reduce their uncertainty (i.e. a new direction to go in). If they have no concept of hypnosis, then the typical pattern interrupt, e.g. a Bandler handshake will be meaningless and thus powerless to them.

However, if they are in a context where you are known to be a hypnotist, then the first stage – attribution – is accounted for. They attribute the interruption of their pattern with reasoning such as, "s/he must be doing something hypnotic... Let's wait and see what happens..." Yet, even then, if you give a suggestion that is meaningless to them, e.g. "you are now under my complete control" (presuming this is undesirable to them or not part of their model of hypnosis), they are not going to follow your lead. They will "snap-out" of their momentary anticipatory trance and find some other way to explain it.

This is not – and this can hardly be stated often enough – magic. Neither is it a way to control another person. It is recognition of the intricate ways that human beings interact with each other.

## The Stages of Kinaesthetic Confusion

It may be useful to think of the hypnotic utilisation of confusion as following a number of steps:

- Interrupt or Overload a Pattern
- Extend the Confusion
- Utilise the Confusion

Please note that all of this relies upon our previously referenced *Anatomy of Inductions*. If you have failed to respect the first element of hypnotic inductions – get consent/contract – then you will fall at the first hurdle. That is, employing the aikido metaphor, unless you have entered their pattern and moved with them, you cannot interrupt it. If you stand on the outside of their pattern and then attempt to interrupt, you will simply be dismissed and they will naturally act to protect themselves from you. Instead, you blend with their movement and join with the pattern. Once again, the Bandler Handshake is an excellent example of this.

You then interrupt or overload their pattern. With the Erickson Handshake, you do both. You physically interrupt them, whilst verbally/mentally overloading them. This leaves them scrambling around for a congruent meaning for this interruption.

The overload does not need to be as convoluted or contrived as many pre-written confusion scripts seem to think. As you are engaging their attention with whatever is happening in their arm, you are merely introducing another (cognitive) element for them to perform, observe or monitor. The words in and of themselves do not make or break the induction, as can be seen with the pantomime version. Yet, they do provide a useful added element to overload your partner. Think of it as throwing a juggler another ball to keep track of.

Finally, you utilise the confusion. If you only interrupted a handshake and then said, "Sleep!" you might not be as successful as you hope. It is generally necessary, to prolong and redirect the pattern. Again, the aikido metaphor is useful here, to slightly modify the three steps above:

- Blend with the pattern (rapport/utilisation)
- Interrupt the pattern (interrupt or overload)
- Extend the pattern (increase/amplify the confusion)

- Redirect the pattern (utilisation)

Mental confusion is often thought of when people discuss confusion inductions. The thing that is often overlooked is that we already have all kinds of physical and/or social patterns that, if interrupted, can create confusion.

A handshake is merely one example. Another example would be a high five. Or, swapping chairs. For example, if you have a client who is fidgety, then you may choose to blend with that pattern by asking them to switch chairs. You might then later ask them to do this again. You can carry on in this way until their "subconscious" mind decides that it no longer wants to jump around in such a manner.

Alternatively, you might notice during calibration, that your client always looks down and to the right when they think of something they don't like. With a quick, "Imagine if..." question, you discover that they look up and to the left if they are imagining something they would like to happen. Consequently, having already discussed something they would like as an outcome, you might choose to distract them – for example, by scratching your head – to look up and to the the left, whilst trying to describe something that troubled them.

Another way that hypnotists utilise kinaesthetic confusion is by rocking their partner's, often as part of a deepening process. It is sometimes suggested that this unbalancing can automatically induce trance. I personally feel that such a perspective takes things too literally. I suspect it is more the case that the rocking is creating a sense of confusion as the client thinks (consciously or otherwise), "I wonder what this means... I guess that something hypnotic is going on..."

One final example would be an arm-levitation. It is possible to achieve this conversationally with someone by simply speaking on their inhalations. I might add a few affirmations – the ubiquitous Ericksonian, "That's right"! - as I see their body rise when they breathe in. When you associate this with a feeling of lightness in your partner's arm, it is not a difficult thing to soon achieve an arm-levitation. However, to our partners it can be incredibly dramatic.

I have had clients pointing to their arm as they ask, astonished, "How is that happening?!" They are 100% certain that they are not lifting their arm, but they can feel and see it lifting. This confusion or disconnect between what is usually expected – the norm, or 'pattern' – and what is experienced in a hypnotic context – the expectation you add to the scenario – is significant. In one well-timed move, you can increase someone's expectation 100-fold.

In my experience, there is something far more compelling about kinaesthetic confusion, compared to mental confusion alone.

## Ambiguous Touch

The key with the Erickson Handshake is simply that your partner will attribute your ambiguous touches to something hypnotic. They just won't know what yet. You can extend this sense of expectant confusion by either carrying on with the ambiguous touches, adding in some mental overload, or asking them to look into your eyes whilst you gaze at them in a confusing way.

At the same time, they will find themselves unsure whether you are holding their arm up, or they are, or if it is staying up on its own. You might amplify this, by pushing up slightly and then allowing it to bounce down. Their tendency will be to keep it up, as that seems to be what you want, which you can of course utilise.

Finally, just as you are removing your hand – either with or without a hand/finger underneath their arm – they are too focused on the mental confusion to worry about whether or not their arm should stay up. Usually, they subconsciously choose to keep it up, giving you leverage to suggest that something hypnotic has happened (extending the pattern) and they can now go into trance (redirection).

A useful way to think of this is to consider channels of information. We receive input through all five of our senses, but also through movement, balance and other channels. With an effective confusion induction, you are not simply speaking in a way that puzzles them. You are acting in such a manner that they are uncertain which channel they can rely upon. This momentary uncertainty is not a familiar or predictable place to stay and most of us will take the earliest viable exit to escape.

As with aikido, a well-performed confusion induction is not a jarring, annoying or obstructive experience. It is, instead, a lot like dancing.

# GRAHAM OLD

# EXERCISE

I would now invite you to go back to the many examples of confusion inductions available for free online.

Consider whether they treat the client's mind as a hindrance to be overcome, or an ally to be utilised.

Practice using the confusion technique, paying attention to the principle of utilisation.

# GRAHAM OLD

# Trouble-Shooting

### They just stare at me after the pattern-interrupt

The number one reason why you may encounter little more than a bemused stare following a pattern-interrupt, is poor timing. This is not a case of being a millisecond out, or failing to flow smoothly like an aikido master. I am talking more about what you do following the pattern interrupt.

If you just stand there, waiting to see if it 'worked,' you will more than likely be disappointed. Your partner is looking for you to provide them with an explanation and direction. If you simply provide a look that says, "Don't ask me, I don't even know if I did it right!" you will soon lose your opportunity.

Just let things flow smoothly. More often than not, even if the pattern interrupt did not 'take,' you will manage to pace and lead your partner if your suggestions are confident and congruent.

### I'm confused by all of the Bandler variations!

That's fine. These are simply arbitrary versions that we compiled for ease of teaching. If it makes a big difference to you to just pick one, then go for it. However, there is something useful as a hypnotist about developing the skill of going with your partner and being able to utilise whatever is offered. So, if their hand ends up way above their head – meaning that gravity is really going to work in your favour – it makes sense to go for a falling hand, even if you initially intended to use frozen hand.

To clarify, we use the following titles to describe the following variations of the Bandler Handshake:

The Floating Hand: Their hand floats up to or towards their face [Think of this as the magnetic forehead!]

The Falling Hand: Their hand falls down to their face (or sometimes their side) [Think of this as the gravity variation!]

The Frozen Hand: Their hand remains cataleptic, in front of their face, where you placed it after the handshake. Usually followed-up with a falling deepener [This is the cataleptic Bandler original]

The Focused Hand: No handshake is used. You simply ask your partner to look at their hand. This can result in either of the three outcomes above [This is Jonathan Chase's "Shapes" version]

The Fast Hand: This is the Derren Brown rapid variation [Think of this as the flashy or face-palm version!].

Nevertheless, these titles or descriptions are not set in

stone. Experiment with what works best for you and those you are working with.

## Won't they feel me pushing their hand?

The first thing to be said is that you are not looking for a direct movement. That is, the intention is not to end up with a hand in front of their face, which you simply push forward. That provides too much movement for your partner to resist against. Instead, aim for more circular movements. This is one of the reasons that we prefer the falling hand, as the hand goes up and over and then down onto their face. The less direct movement gives less cause for resistance.

Nevertheless, the second thing to note is that they will only object to you pushing their hand if they don't want it to happen. So, if you have given them no idea that their arm will move, if they sensed you pushing their hand they might object. Or, if you have implied that their hand will move all on its own, if they feel you pushing it they may conclude that you are trying to fool them.

So, this is only an issue to be concerned about if your actions do not match your words. After all, if you look at the fast hand variation, the hand is very much pushed right up to their face. If you move smoothly, explaining what will happen – and what is happening – then this is not something you need to excessively worry about.

## What do I say when I'm pointing at their hand?

Anthony Jacquin provides a succinct and effective script

to use if you are concerned about how to direct their attention to the hand in front of their face:

> Look at your hand
> Look at the lines on it
> Look at one spot...

It really can be as simple as that!

## They resist my pattern-interrupt

On occasions, you will come up against someone who intentionally resists you trying to transform a handshake into a hand up in front of their face. There are a couple of reasons why this may be.

Firstly, you are opposing their natural movement. Once again, this comes down to avoiding direct oppositional movements in favour of circular blending ones.

Additionally, someone trained in martial arts – particularly Aikido, Ju-Jitsu, Wing Chun or Tai Chi – may be highly sensitive to variations in touch, particularly around their wrist and forearm. In that case, the Bandler Handshake is not the most appropriate induction to use, unless you opt for the focused hand variation, or have a high pain threshold!

If your partner is resisting, it may be because they sense something unusual is happening – which, from your perspective, is the whole point! – and they do not realise that it is part of the hypnosis.

I see absolutely no reason to hypnotise someone without at least some level of agreement. So, a useful pre-talk can eradicate multitudes of problems that unexpected or impromptu hypnosis can cause. Part of your pre-talk can even include something like, "I may touch your hand, arm or shoulder at different points and in different ways, that's all part of the magic. [Smile] Okay?" You then have consent to touch them, as well as an expectation from them that if you go on to touch them on the hand/arm in strange ways, it is all part of the process.

When they agree, you can say, "Thanks, I appreciate that..." as you go to shake their hand.

## Their arm is heavy and does not stay up

Your best option here is to adjust your technique, utilising their response to opt for a different outcome.

A key-phrase to use when things do not go according to plan can empower your client, without implying that they have managed to resist you or that you cannot achieve any results with them. The phrase I commonly use is something like:

> "Well, I can see that your subconscious is alert and active. [Smile] ...And we can use that... So, let's do this another way... You've got this."

As you can see, I imply that we are changing approaches not because what I did failed, or because they could not do what was expected. Instead, I simply attribute it to their 'active' or powerful subconscious. Yet, without suggesting failure, my final three words - "You've got this" - could be taken to imply that success this time around depends on them responding differently.

You can then switch from one handshake induction to another, or – and this may be particularly relevant as the 'heaviness' of the hand was an issue – you can switch from frozen hand to falling hand. This entails ensuring that you bring their hand round high enough, so that it is above their eye-line. If you get the angle correct, then you will naturally have a float-to-the-face or fall to the side effect. Failing all else, opt for the focused hand variation.

## They do not close their eyes during Elman

Were you clear in your initial instructions/suggestions? It can help to get an explicit agreement from them that they have understood. Additionally, I have found that it helps to nod as you shake, to confirm what they should do.

However, there is no point carrying on to the 3rd shake, if they are clearly not even responding to the first one. In this case, you do not want to imply failure on anyone's part. Instead, you will change your shake from single to continuous, or vice-versa as you go through the directions again. Your patter may sound something like this, as you give the impression that this is an experiment that you are both working on and with which you are both interested in the results and determined to succeed.

> "Well, I can see that your subconscious is alert and active. [Smile] ...And we can use that... So, I suspect that we will have more success if we do it this way..."

[Explain the process again, with an alternate type of shaking. As you state what they will do each time, nod your head. This will often elicit a nod from them, confirming that they understand.]

"You've got this."

Notice that you are direct this time, even if you were permissive the first time around.

## It [whichever handshake] is still not working!

You may now want to consider your general approach. Are you setting-up a challenge, that they either resist or feel they cannot live up to? Are you being too permissive, or too direct?

You can switch to another induction, such as another handshake, or something related like the 8-word hand-drop. However, if you choose to use a non-arm-based induction (perhaps because your confidence has taken a slight temporary dip), you do not want to switch immediately as it will give the impression that things have failed irretrievably.

Instead, pick up their heavy arm by the wrist, shake it slightly and say something along the lines of:

"In a moment, I am going to *let go* of this heavy arm. And as I do so, I want you to allow your eyes to close as you go inside and relax."

[Lift the arm slightly and then drop it by their side. If they do not close their eyes, go direct and say:]

"So, go ahead and close your eyes as you go inside and let go of any stress and tension.

"And just carry on breathing in that way... [said on the inhale] breathing-in peace and calm and [said on the exhale] letting go of all stress and tension..."

[If they did close their eyes, carry on by saying:]

"In a moment, not yet, but in a moment, I am going to pick-up your other arm, limp, loose and relaxed, and when I do, you can take a nice deep breath. Then, as I *let go*, you can go even deeper into that relaxation, letting go, floating, drifting deeper down..."

[Pick up their other arm, shaking it slightly slowly from side to side. If they do not take a breath, say, "now taking a nice deep breath." Then let the arm go and regardless of their response, say, "That's right..."]

"And I would like you to take a moment now to simply be. Your subconscious is learning to work in new ways, for your benefit, and there is no need for us to rush that... So, when you are ready, when your subconscious and conscious mind are ready to work together to embrace new learnings, employ fresh resources and take you to new depths of experience, you can open your eyes and we will continue..."

# THE HYPNOTIC HANDSHAKES

You are now in a better position to carry on with any induction you choose. As inductions with a strong physical element have not yet signified success to the two of you, you could carry on deepening the relaxation with a simple progressive muscle relaxation. Another way to proceed with their current level of relaxation and morph it into a hypnotic induction, would be something like *Dr. Flower's Induction* seen in Appendix B.

However, my suggestion, depending on why you feel they have not responded as expected, would be to opt for an induction without any element of binary challenge or failure. I am not in your shoes, so it is difficult to judge the impact of the previous non-successes, or to ascertain how well you have re-framed them as feedback to discover the best way to work with their powerful subconscious mind. Nevertheless, if you sense any feeling of failure on their part, or scepticism of your abilities, it would be wise to avoid switching to an induction that has a succeed/fail element to it, e.g. an eye-lock or arm-levitation. An obvious example would be something like *the Leisure Induction*, which we just happen to have released a previous title on in this very series!

If you act smoothly and confidently during this entire process, then you will often find that your partner presumes all of the handshakes were merely information-gathering techniques. You, however, know that they eventually became useful pre-frames and provided you with a workable level of relaxation before you even began your 'real' induction.

## I am too nervous to use Erickson's Handshake!

Erickson's ambiguous touch does seem to generate its own unique insecurities in some hypnotists. Whether it is the direct eye-gaze, or the presumed clever patter, or the risk that their arm will just fall down, this handshake is often the least practised of the three. And that's a real shame, because it's a whole lot of fun!

My confidence-boosting tip – besides, "Practice! Practice! Practice!" - is a little phrase which edges the bets in your favour. Just as you are letting the arm go, simply say, "And that can just stay right there for now..." There are a number of ways to use this, depending on how the induction is proceeding:

> "And that can just stay right there for now, as you take a nice deep breath and allow your eyes to close..."

Or:

> "And that can just stay right there for now, as if it were floating in mid-air, fully aware that both it and you are preparing to float down into a nice hypnotic state..."

And so on!

## They ALWAYS end up with heavy arms!

You may find that whether you are using the Bandler or Erickson handshake, you always encounter the same problem – heavy arms! This may be down to your technique, though it is more likely to do with the level of confidence and congruence that you are projecting. Or, it may simply be a run of bad luck!

Either way, a useful way to proceed, at least until this stops being a regular problem, is to use two hands. You have no doubt seen people, usually in Business, who hold their partner's forearm with one hand, whilst their other hand does the shaking. This is something you can utilise. In fact, with Bandler, it can be perfectly natural to end up with one hand holding their hand up, whilst your other hand is under their elbow.

It is useful not to be too constrained by instructions regarding the correct way to do these inductions (even those found in this book). That will only add pressure and make things seem forced. It is more natural to flow with what feels most natural to you. Yet, in this instance, I would recommend the two-armed approach, which can feel just as natural as a one-handed handshake.

You then gradually let go of the arm, a bit from the top, a bit from the bottom, then apply ambiguous pressure here and there, until they are left not knowing who is keeping their arm up. With practice, you will feel when they 'take' the arm. This is usually a subconscious decision on their part. Either way, you carry on as if everything is taking place as expected.


## What about people with power handshakes?

Talking of people with two-armed handshakes, what about those people who never shake hands naturally? Donald Trump is an obvious example, yet many Business people have similar habits. They may pull you towards them, twist your arm round so their hand is on top, or clasp one of your hands between two of theirs.

My suggestion with such people is to let them have their power shake. Obviously, their fragile egos require it. Then, having shaken hands, I might point to their other hand and say, "Actually, can I borrow that hand?" I would then proceed with a focused hand induction.

Asking to borrow the hand bypasses any sense of competition. You are acknowledging that it is their arm and they are in charge of it, but you are asking them to momentarily place it in your care. Additionally, I usually point to the hand they did not shake with, but this is not necessary. The reason I do it is that they are used to being in control of their other arm and do all manner of twists and turns with it to come out on top. So, to avoid any possible conflict in their mind, I skip it completely and just opt to use their non-shaking hand.

## Why do you not teach an arm-pull?

A somewhat popular handshake induction, which we have avoided completely is the arm-pull. You will likely have seen this on the internet or even television. It simply involves the hypnotist pulling their 'subject's' arm whilst giving the sleep command.

We have intentionally not covered this induction for a number of reasons. Firstly, it is difficult to teach such an induction safely within the confines of a book.

Secondly, related to the above, we have rarely seen this induction carried out with sufficient attention given to health and/or safety concerns. Some hypnotists will check that their subject does not have any shoulder, or back complaints, but neither they nor their subject are medical professionals. To be sure that the induction is safe, they need to ask about hand, wrist, elbow, shoulder, neck and back injuries. Additionally, they should probably enquire as to their subject's heart condition as well!

Thirdly, an arm-pull is almost always abrasive and shocking and – as such – completely unnecessary. Surprise is enough to achieve hypnosis. Shock is not needed. Inductions of this type only serve to perpetuate the stereotype that the hypnotist is the all-powerful master and his subject is merely a pawn in his hands. We much prefer a straightforward pattern-interrupt that can convey skilful delivery if needed, but also highlights the complexity and flexibility of your partner's mind.

## Where can I learn more?

Well, howtodoinductions.com, of course! Sign-up there for our newsletter, where we keep folks up to date with news about the site, upcoming trainings, new books and the occasional tips and techniques.

# GRAHAM OLD

# EXERCISE

Continue to practice the handshake inductions taught in this book.

When using the Bandler handshake, practice the "flow-chart" approach of moving from one variation to another, depending on your partner's responses.

Practice the Elman Handshake. As you progress with it, play around with what you suggest will happen with each shake.

When you use Erickson's Handshake, practice with both verbal and not-so-verbal variations. Practice different means of overloading the mind, whilst you ambiguously touch their hand.

Contact us at howtodoinductions.com if you have any questions which we have not yet answered.

# GRAHAM OLD

# Bibliography

Battino, R & South, T. (2005). *Ericksonian Approaches: A Comprehensive Manual.* Carmarthen: Crown House.

Battino, R. (2006). *Expectation: The Very Brief Therapy Book.* Carmarthen: Crown House Publishing.

Dobson, Terry, and Riki Moss. (1993). *It's a Lot like Dancing: An Aikido Journey.* Berkeley, CA: Frog.

Erickson, M. H. (1976). *Hypnotic Realities: The Induction of Clinical Hypnosis and Forms of Indirect Suggestion.* New York: Irvington Publishers.

Erickson, M.H., and Ross, E.L. (1976). 'Two-level communication and the microdynamics of trance and suggestion.' *American Journal of Clinical Hypnosis, 18.*

Gilligan, S. G. (1987). *Therapeutic Trances: The Co-Operation Principle In Ericksonian Hypnotherapy.* New York: Routledge.

Jacquin, A. (2007). *Reality is Plastic.* Derby: UKHTC.

Kirsch, I. (1990). *Changing Expectations: A key to*

*effective psychotherapy*. Pacific Grove, CA: Brooks/Cole

Lynn, Steven J., and Irving Kirsch. (2006). *Essentials of Clinical Hypnosis: An Evidence-based Approach*. Washington, DC: American Psychological Association.

Lynn, S. & Rhue, J. Eds. (1991) *Theories of Hypnosis: Current Models and Perspectives*. New York: Guilford Press.

Michael, Garry & Kirsch, (2012). 'Suggestion, Cognition and Behavior.' In: *Current Directions in Psychological Science* 2.

Nash, M. & Barnier, A., eds. (2008). *The Oxford Handbook of Hypnosis: Theory, Research, and Practice*. Oxford: OUP.

Old, G. (2014). *Mastering the Leisure Induction*. Milton Keynes: Plastic Spoon.

Old, G. (2017). *The Elman Induction*. Milton Keynes: Plastic Spoon.

Rossi, E. L. (Ed.) (1980). *The collected papers of Milton H. Erickson, Volume 1: The nature of hypnosis and suggestions*. New York: Irvington.

Strozzi-Heckler, Richard. (1985). *Aikido And The New Warrior*. 1st ed. Berkeley, Calif.: North Atlantic Books.

Yapko, M. (2003). *Trancework: An Introduction to the Practice of Clinical Hypnosis.* New York: Routledge.

# APPENDIX A – The PII Induction

The PII Induction, or the *Pattern-Interrupt Interrupt,* is a unique induction perfect for use with those who would be expecting a pattern-interrupt.

We first devised this induction for use in training situations, when it is almost impossible to deliver a pattern interrupt, whilst teaching about pattern interrupts! The solution was rather obvious – simply interrupt in a different way.

Here is a transcript of a time when we were teaching the Bandler Handshake, but interrupted to morph into a far less dramatic ambiguous touch.

> Hypnotist: "So, just to re-cap, we will go into a handshake like this..."
>
> [Hypnotist offers their hand, to which the participant responds by putting their own hand forward.]
>
> H: "And just as our hands are about to touch, my other hand comes forward, grabs their wrist and moves the hand up here..."
>
> [The hypnotist performs the first stage of a typical floating hand Bandler handshake.]

# GRAHAM OLD

H: "Got it?" [Participant nods.]

Hypnotist: "So, just so everyone can see, we will go into a handshake like this..."

[Hypnotist offers their hand, to which the participant still automatically responds by putting their own hand forward.]

H: "Then, just as our hands are about to touch, my other hand comes forward and takes their wrist and moves the hand up here..."

[Hypnotist lets their hand go, steps back and steps forward again...]

H: "So, one last time, because I want to make absolutely sure we've all got this, we will go to shake hands..."

[This time the hypnotist does not remove their hand, but meets their participant's hand and shakes it. The speed of the shake slows down as the hypnotist says:]

H: "And you know exactly how quickly you can access that deeper resourceful state, as you go down inside you..."

[The handshake has slowed down such that it has now almost stopped.]

H: "And you don't need to close your eyes until

136

you are ready to fully enter that state..."

[Participant's eyes close.]

H: "And discover all of those learnings that have been waiting for you deep..."

[Hypnotist lets go of participant's hand, which remains cataleptic...]

H: "...deep inside you.

"That's right... Go all the way down... Calm, comfortable, safe and serene... that natural place where your subconscious mind has already begun to learn those lessons and make all of those connections to where you need to go.

"And only as quickly as your subconscious and conscious mind can agree together to work for your good... will that hand begin to drift down now, taking you deeper... that's it... all the way..."

As you will see, the possibilities here are endless. You simply set up a pattern-interrupt as a new pattern and then interrupt it any way you choose.
Have fun!

# GRAHAM OLD

# APPENDIX B – Dr. Flower's Induction

Hypnotist: "I would like you to start, by picking a point on that wall, where you can focus all of your attention.

"Look at that wall, almost as if you can see through to a perfect calm and soothing scene. You may even feel like you are looking into a daydream. Either way, simply rest your eyes on one spot on that wall."

[Wait until your partner's eyes appear to have fixed on one spot, ideally appearing slightly defocused.]

"That's right. Now, bring *all* of your attention to that spot, as you rest your eyes there.

"Soon you'll find all of the muscle groups in your body will relax. Your facial muscles will relax. Your arms will relax. Your legs will relax. Your whole body will let go.

"And soon you will close your eyes... and go into a sound, peaceful hypnotic rest.

"Hypnosis is not a state of unconsciousness, but rather a state of dreamy relaxation where the mind is open to new experiences.

"Are you ready?"

Partner: "Yeah."

H: "In a moment, I am going to count backwards from 20 to one. With each number I say, you will close your eyes. And in between the counts, you'll open them.

"So, for example: 20 – close...open. 19 – close...open. 18 – close...open. And so on.

"And what you will begin to notice is that it increasingly feels like too much effort to open your eyes. You would rather keep them closed, enjoying that scene, over there, drifting into that experience.

"And sometime before I reach 1, maybe at five, maybe at ten, maybe even at fifteen... You'll close your eyes and go into deep, sound hypnotic rest.

"Okay?"

P: "Yep."

H: "Perfect. Let's begin."

"20... 19... 18...

"Notice now how easily you can sink into this process, just allowing yourself to enjoy that experience...

"As you begin to feel that relaxation spreading throughout your body..."

[Partner's facial muscles relax and drop.]

"That's right.

"17... 16... 15...

"And you can be aware of that sense of relaxation, and as you do you can notice how it becomes more and more inconvenient to open those eyes...

"14... 13..."

[The hypnotist notices their partner struggling to open their eyes, so interrupts the usual pattern of counting in threes...]

"And when it becomes too difficult to open them, or just too easy to keep them closed, you can keep them closed; simply imagining that you are opening them.

"12...

"That relaxation spreading throughout your body, as you drift deeper into that rest. And the deeper you go, the better you feel... and the better you feel, the deeper you go.

"11... 10..."

[The partner does not open their eyes between 11 and 10.]

"That's right.

"9... 8... 7...

"Enjoying that deep deep rest...

"6... 5... 4...

"And with each number now, you can find that relaxation doubling, going deeper down, twice as deep.

"3... 2... 1...

"That's it... Any remaining stress or tension, just disappearing, evaporating from your body...

"And in a moment, not yet but in a moment, I am going to say the number "zero." And you can even picture that big round number in front of you... like the 'O' in the word, 'hypnosis.' And when I say that number, you will move through into deep hypnosis... completely relaxed in mind and body... stepping into that calm and soothing space your own mind has created for you...

"Get ready...

"Zero...

"And you go straight through that big round number, stepping into a deep hypnotic rest... as you let go all the way down..."

# GRAHAM OLD

# APPENDIX C – Expectancy Inductions

The following expectancy induction transcripts are reproduced with kind permission of John Cleesatel.

> Hypnotist: "In a moment, I will say the names of some colours. I won't let you know what colours I am going to say, but when I say the first colour, you will notice a nice warm glow in your chest. It will be very soothing and will feel very good. Let me know when you feel this, and we will move on.
>
> H: "Is that ok with you?"
>
> Partner: "Yep."
>
> H: "Are you ready?"
>
> P: [nods]
>
> H: "Green."
>
> [Hypnotist snaps their fingers and then waits for their partner to tell them they feel it.]
>
> P: "I feel it."

H: "Feels good doesn't it."

P: [nods]

H: "Are we ready to move on?"

P: [nods]

H: "Okay, when I say the next colour, you will notice this warm glow will spread all over your body, relaxing you very much and feeling absolutely wonderful.

"You will notice that your eyelids have become very heavy.

"It is up to you if you close them or not, but you will find it is much easier to relax if you do.

"When you feel this, let me know and we will proceed.

"Is that okay with you?"

P: "Yep."

H: "Good... Are you ready?"

P: "Yep."

H: "Blue."

[Hypnotist snaps their fingers and then waits for

their partner to tell them they feel it.]

P: "Ok."

H: "Are we ready to move on?"

P: [nods]

H: "Good... When I say the next colour, you will notice your eye-lids are so relaxed that they will no longer open.

"When you are sure they are that relaxed, I want you to try to open them, and give them a good try. You will notice that the harder you try to open them, the more firmly they remain closed.

"Is that okay with you?"

P: [nods]

H: "Good... Are you ready?"

P: [nods]

H: "Purple."

[Hypnotist snaps their fingers and then waits for them to test their eyes...]

H: "That's good, now stop trying and feel yourself drifting deeper into trance...Notice how good that feels... That's it."

## Expectancy Induction 2

Hypnotist: "So, I'd like to tell you first, that there's no way you can help me. Trance is about automatic reaction, not wilful compliance. So, it's kinda like a hiccough or a sneeze. It's not something that you can make happen, but you can notice it when it does. And that's what I'm gonna ask you to do.

"Are you right or left-handed?"

Partner: "I'm right-handed."

H: "Okay, so what I'm gonna do is, if it's okay with you, I'd like to hypnotise your left arm, whilst you watch."

P: "Alright."

H: "Would that be a cool thing to do?"

P: "Sure."

H: "Okay. Now, if you would, just kinda let your arm loose, try not to lean any weight on it or anything. And for a few moments, I'll take control of your arm. Is that okay?"

P: "Okay."

H: "That's great. Now, remember that there's no way you can help me. There's nothing that you *need* to do, other than to let me know when you feel it. So, I'm gonna ask you actually to play scientist or news reporter, if you will. Monitor how your arm feels and let me know when you feel what I suggest. Is that ok?"

P: "That's good."

H: "Okay, great. Now in a moment, I'm gonna say the name of a colour. When I say the colour, you're gonna notice that your left arm starts feeling very relaxed and it's gonna start feeling very heavy.

"Is that ok with you?"

P: "That's okay."

H: "And when you notice this, just let me know by saying, 'I feel it.' Are you ready?

P: "I'm ready"

H: "Here we go... Blue."

P: "I feel it."

H: "Okay. Now in a moment, I'm gonna say another colour and when I do you're gonna notice that that relaxation feeling, that heaviness is gonna become much more profound, its going to become much stronger. It's gonna feel really good. Is that alright?"

P: "That's ok."

H: "Are you ready?"

P: "I'm ready."

H: "Let me know when you feel it again by saying I feel it. Green."

P: "I feel it."

H: "Ok. Now in a moment I'll say one more colour. When I say this colour, you're gonna notice that your arm becomes so totally and perfectly relaxed. So completely and utterly heavy that its not gonna want to move. As a matter of fact, the harder you try to move your arm, the more its just gonna sit there and do nothing, and the deeper in trance it's gonna take you.

"Is that ok with you?"

P: "That's ok."

H: "Are you ready? "

P: "Im ready."

H: "Purple... Now, when you're absolutely sure that your arm is so totally and completely relaxed and so heavy that it won't move, I'm gonna ask you to try it, to test it and I want you to give it a good test. But you're gonna notice the harder you try to move it, the more it is not gonna move and the deeper into trance it will take you. So, give yourself a moment, give it a good test and when you're sure it wont move just left me know and we'll move on."

[Shuffles upper body, as if trying to lift arm up.]

H: "You can use your other hand, if you'd like, to help."

[Uses other arm to try and lift left arm, to no avail.]

H: "How's that?"

P: "Okay."

H: "Okay. So, notice your arm moves perfectly well just now..."

[Clicks fingers.]

H: "...just like it did before. Go ahead, check it out."

[Client lifts her left hand off of the chair.]

H: "Now is that cool, or what?"

P: "That's cool!"

# GRAHAM OLD

## APPENDIX D – Bandler Flowchart

**Does Their Hand End-up High?**

Yes

No

Is it light or responsive?

Is it heavy or rigid?

Yes

No

Yes

No

Falling Hand (or frozen)

Falling to side (or frozen with support)

Focused hand (with support) Or falling to side

Frozen Hand (or floating) (or focused)

# GRAHAM OLD

# About the Author

**Graham Old** is a Solution-focused Hypnotist from the United Kingdom. A Graduate of Spurgeon's College, London and the University of Wales, Graham is a former University Chaplain and Community Pastor and remains an active participant of local peace and justice campaigns. He has experience as a Father's Worker and Assistant Social Worker, as well as working in private clinical practice and running the most popular inductions site on the web.

Graham is a popular conference speaker, writer and trainer, with over two decades experience teaching meditation and self-hypnosis. He is an insightful presence in contemporary hypnosis and the developer of the acclaimed *Therapeutic Inductions* approach.

# GRAHAM OLD

# THE HYPNOTIC HANDSHAKES

www.ingramcontent.com/pod-product-compliance
Lightning Source LLC
Chambersburg PA
CBHW070833310526
45788CB00017B/562